MW00435718

POTENTIAL IN THE

PALM

OF YOUR HAND

REVEAL YOUR HIDDEN
TALENTS THROUGH PALMISTRY

About the Author

Richard Webster was born and raised in New Zealand. He has been interested in the psychic world since he was nine years old. As a teenager, he became involved in hypnotism and later became a professional stage hypnotist. After school, he worked in the publishing business and purchased a bookstore. The concept of reincarnation played a significant role in his decision to become a past-life specialist. Richard has also taught psychic development classes, which are based on many of his books.

Richard's first book was published in 1972, fulfilling a childhood dream of becoming an author. Richard is now the author of over a hundred books and is still writing today. His bestselling books include *Spirit Guides & Angel Guardians* and *Creative Visualization for Beginners*.

Richard has appeared on several radio and TV programs in the United States and abroad. He currently resides in New Zealand with his wife and three children. He regularly travels the world to give lectures, hold workshops, and continue his research.

POTENTIAL IN THE
PALM
OF YOUR HAND

REVEAL YOUR HIDDEN
TALENTS THROUGH PALMISTRY

RICHARD WEBSTER

Llewellyn Publications
Woodbury, Minnesota

FIRST EDITION
First Printing, 2019

Cover design by Shannon McKuhen
Editing: by Brian R. Erdrich
Interior art by Llewellyn Art Department

Llewellyn Publications is a registered trademark of Llewellyn Worldwide Ltd.

Library of Congress Cataloging-in-Publication Data (Pending)
ISBN: 978-0-7387-5969-2

Llewellyn Publications
A Division of Llewellyn Worldwide Ltd.
2143 Wooddale Drive
Woodbury, MN 55125-2989
www.llewellyn.com

Printed in the United States of America

Other Books by Richard Webster

Forthcoming Books by Richard Webster

For my good friend and fellow palmist, Jesse James

Contents

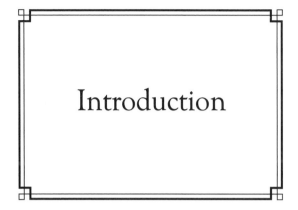

Introduction

I became interested in palmistry when I was ten years old. We had recently moved to a new house and one of our neighbors was well known in the community because of her baking skills. I got to know her as quickly as I could and regularly visited her and her husband. They were a middle-aged, childless couple who very much enjoyed my visits. At least once a week I'd sit in their library eating her baking and looking at their books. I was a keen reader and it was exciting to meet people who actually had a library room in their home.

One day I discovered a large section of books on palmistry. The husband was a palmist and he started teaching me the basics of the art. I used to enjoy looking at the hands of friends at school, but it didn't mean much until puberty hit and I discovered how useful palmistry was when it came to meeting girls. It must have been about that time that someone asked me what sort of career I thought he should go into once he left school. Consequently, he may well have unintentionally motivated me to start researching this book when I was just fifteen or sixteen years old.

In the early 1980s, I used to spend one week a month reading palms in shopping malls. The malls booked me as entertainment, and because of this, the readings had to be positive and no more than five minutes long. The point of the exercise was to send people away with a smile on their faces in the hope that it would encourage them to spend more money in the mall.

The readings were extremely popular, and I always had a line of people waiting for a reading. I read hundreds of palms every week. Every now and again, I read a hand that revealed a significant talent. When I pointed these traits out, some of my clients said they were unaware of them, while others said they knew of their talents, but for one reason or another, had done nothing to develop them. It was sad to learn that so many people were living their lives unaware of, or making virtually no use of, their special gifts.

Fortunately, a few people acted on my suggestions. One I particularly remember was a woman in her middle twenties who had a talent for singing. When I pointed this out, she laughed and told me she'd enjoyed singing at school and was often chosen whenever a soloist was required. When she left school, her parents refused to let her take it further, as they didn't think she'd be able to have a successful career in music. Instead, she'd trained as a beauty therapist—a career she enjoyed but didn't love.

I met her again a couple of years later. She came back for another reading and told me she'd decided to follow her dream. She was in the chorus of a musical that was touring the country and was the understudy for the leading role. After that, I followed her career with interest as she ultimately left the chorus and built up a successful career in musicals and light opera. She's still singing professionally, and I've spoken to her on several occasions over the years. Each time she thanks me for pointing out the singing talents that are shown on her palm.

Over the years, I've spoken to a number of other people who started pursuing their special skills and talents at least partly because of the reading I'd given them. Of course, they are the exceptions, and most people probably continued along the path they were already on after having had a reading from me.

It's sad to see so much potential wasted, and I've written this book for anyone who feels they might have a latent gift or talent that they could develop. I believe everyone has a gift of some sort, and the happiest people are those who can turn whatever it happens to be into a career or vocation. If you're searching for your special talent, I hope this book will help you find it.

Chapter One

The Shape
of the Hand

People have been fascinated with hands for thousands of years. Handprints can be found in many ancient Stone Age cave paintings. Palmistry also has an extremely old history. The Bible contains at least three references to palmistry: "He sealeth up the hand of every man; that all men may know his work" (King James Version, Job 37:7), "What evil *is* in mine hand?" (1 Samuel 26:18), and "Length of days *is* in her right hand; *and* in her left hand riches and honor" (Proverbs 3:16). The mudras, or symbolic hand gestures, that are used in Hinduism and Buddhism are believed to be at least five thousand years old.

Over two thousand years ago, Aristotle, the ancient Greek philosopher, wrote about palmistry in his book *De Historia Animalium*. One of his observations was that people with long lines on their palms tended to live longer than people with shorter lines.

"Modern" palmistry began in the nineteenth century when two Frenchmen became interested in the subject. Stanislas d'Arpentigny (1798–1861), a retired army officer, lived close to a wealthy landowner who was fascinated with the latest advances in science. The landowner's wife was interested in the arts. Both of them held weekly parties for their friends. D'Arpentigny was interested in both science and the arts and used to be invited to both parties. He was intrigued to discover that the landowner's scientific friends had fingers with knotted joints, whilst his wife's artistic friends had hands with smooth fingers. This chance discovery encouraged him to study the subject and he ultimately wrote a book about his findings called *La Cheirognomie*, which was published in 1843.

At the same time, Adolphe Desbarolles (1801–1886), a well-known portrait painter, started studying palmistry to see if he could update "a science as old as the world." His book, *Les Mysteres de la Main*, was published in 1860.

A few decades later, William G. Benham, an American palmist, published his monumental book *The Laws of Scientific Hand Reading* in 1900. Since then, advances in psychology, medicine, and the study of skin ridge patterns have totally changed traditional palmistry, and today it's being used to help people in many different ways that have nothing to do with fate or fortune.

The Major and Minor Hands

The major, or dominant, hand is the hand the person uses naturally. This is the right hand for someone who is right-handed, and the left hand for a person who is left-handed.

Until the middle of the twentieth century, palmists believed that the major hand revealed what the person was doing with his or her life, while the other hand revealed the skills and talents the person was born with. However, as both hands change as the person progresses through life, this cannot be correct. Nowadays, the major hand is thought to reveal what the person is doing with his or her life, while the minor hand shows what he or she is thinking about. The minor hand still reveals the person's potentials, but it gradually changes to reveal what the person would like to be doing. In many cases, this can be completely different to what the person is doing in his or her everyday life. If, for instance, someone was working as a clerk in an insurance company but really wanted to be an airplane pilot, there would be major differences between his or her right and left palms.

This is why it's important to examine both hands when giving someone a palm reading. If I'm giving quick readings of the type I used to do in shopping malls, I have time to read only the major hand. However, I always examine both hands when giving someone a serious reading.

Texture of the Skin

The skin texture reveals how people function in everyday life. Someone with fine, silky skin would be happier and more successful dealing with beautiful works of art than, for instance, working as a builder, plumber, or electrician. Someone with coarse skin would be the opposite. Skin texture is determined by examining the back of the hand. Some people have skin that is fine and smooth, while others have skin that is rougher and coarser.

People with fine skin texture are sensitive, gentle, refined, and empathetic. They can be easily hurt or offended by anything that disturbs their sensitive natures. They appreciate beauty and want their home and work environments to be as attractive as possible. They prefer to work indoors rather than outside.

Hard physical work does not create coarse hands, even though it can produce calluses. Coarse hands have highly obvious pores in the skin. People with coarse hands are energetic, down-to-earth, and direct. They usually enjoy good health. They have simple needs and are perfectly happy as long as these needs are met.

They're also "thick-skinned." People with coarse skin are rough and ready and have a down-to-earth approach to everything they do. They say what's on their minds and are less emotional and less high-strung than people with a fine skin texture.

Consistency

Consistency is determined by pressing gently on the palms of the hands. You'll find some hands are hard and resistant to pressure, while others are soft and spongy. Most people's palms are somewhere between these two extremes.

People with soft and spongy palms function best in comfortable surroundings where they can do as little as possible. They lack energy and tend to be lazy and frivolous. People with fleshy palms enjoy partaking in the luxuries of life and are likely to overindulge whenever an opportunity arises.

People with firmer palms are energetic, practical, and enjoy challenges. They work hard and are happiest when they're busy. People with firmer palms are able to avoid overindulging if something else appears to be more important at the time. These people are motivated and persistent. Consequently, they're better able to handle the ups and downs of life than people with fleshy palms.

Flexibility

There is a direct correlation between the flexibility of someone's mind and the flexibility of his or her palm. People with flexible palms are adaptable and can change direction in an instant. People with rigid hands are inflexible, stubborn, and unyielding.

To determine the flexibility of someone's hand, rest the back of the palm on your fingers and press downward on his or her fingertips with your thumb. Most people's hands will bend down slightly, but you'll also find others that are totally unyielding, as well as some that bend back easily.

You can also test each fingertip individually to determine how resistant they are to pressure. The thumb should also be checked to see how firm it is. If it bends back easily, the person will give in under pressure. If the thumb is stiff, the person will be stubborn and unyielding.

Hand Types

Hands can be classified in different ways. Captain Stanislas d'Arpentigny classified the hand into six types: elementary, spatulate, square, knotty, conic, and psychic (d'Arpentigny, 1843). Because this didn't cover everyone, he later added a seventh type called mixed. His classification was useful in the mid nineteenth century, but is less useful nowadays, as hands have changed to reflect increased education and the world we live in today.

The simplest system divides the hand into two types: intuitive and practical. The intuitive hand is long and slim and usually has numerous fine lines on the palm. People with intuitive hands are gentle, thoughtful, idealistic, easily hurt, and sensitive. They enjoy coming up with good ideas but find it hard to put them into action. The palm of the intuitive hand is oblong.

The practical hand is broader and conveys strength, energy, and activity. People with practical hands are logical, capable, and use thoughts more than hunches or feelings. They have the ability to start something and take it all the way to completion. The palm of the practical hand is square.

There are numerous other systems, some containing up to thirteen different types of hands.

No system is perfect, as every hand is different. The system that is most popular today divides the hands into four groups, known as earth, air, fire, and water. This uses square- and oblong-shaped palms, as well as short and long fingers, to create the four possibilities.

Square Palm

A square palm is broad and square or slightly oblong in shape. People with square palms are practical, capable, and down-to-earth. The broadness of the palm provides them with plenty of stamina and energy. They can work hard for long periods when necessary. They have a positive approach to life.

Oblong Palm

An oblong palm is longer in length than it is in breadth. People with oblong palms get bored easily and need plenty of variety in their lives. They are imaginative and come up with good ideas, but sometimes lack the necessary motivation and energy to get them started.

Finger Length

The length of the fingers is determined by their length in proportion to the palm. Usually it's easy to determine long or short fingers, but there are exceptions. If you're finding it hard to decide, ask the person to fold his or her fingers over the palm. If the fingers reach more than seven-eighths of the way down the palm, they're said to be long. Unfortunately, this system isn't perfect, as some people have flexible hands and fingers, and can reach further down the palm than people with more rigid hands and fingers. If you can't determine if the fingers are long or short, they're classified as being medium in length. The best way to determine the lengths of palms and fingers is by taking palm prints (see chapter 12).

Short Fingers

People with short fingers are restless and impatient. They enjoy being busy, think quickly, and can work simultaneously on a number of different tasks. They prefer the overall view, and dislike details. They start everything they do with great enthusiasm but tend to lose interest before the task is completed.

Long Fingers

People with long fingers are patient and enjoy anything that is involved and detailed. They enjoy finishing what they start. They are conscientious, responsible, and like to understand all the fine details of anything they're involved with.

Medium Fingers

People with fingers that are neither long nor short possess a mixture of the qualities possessed by both long and short fingered people. They might, for instance, be patient most of the time, but can also surprise others by acting impatiently on other occasions. They're generally responsible people who like to finish what they start, but they can be overly hasty, and rush something if it doesn't particularly interest them.

It can be useful to observe finger lengths in everyday life. Most of the time you'll find people with longer fingers in roles that involve details, such as dealing with facts or figures, handling money, or involved in a technical industry. Short-fingered people often prefer working with their hands or in any field where their ability to make quick decisions is required. Interestingly, people with both short and long fingers make good entrepreneurs.

Earth, Air, Fire, and Water

We can now combine the two different types of palms (square and oblong) with the two types of fingers (short and long) to create four combinations: a square palm with short fingers, a square palm with long fingers, an oblong palm with short fingers, and an oblong palm with long fingers.

It's important to note that this system divides all of humanity into four groups. Consequently, you'll find many hands that do not fit neatly into any particular group, and you might need to take palm prints that you can measure to determine which group a particular person fits into.

Earth Hand

The earth hand consists of a square palm with short fingers. Earth hands usually have few lines on them, though they are deep and well-marked. People with earth hands enjoy keeping busy and working with their hands. They are practical, reliable, responsible, cautious, and solid. They can also be impatient, critical, distrustful, and change moods in an instant. They enjoy a quiet lifestyle and prefer to live well away from the noise and bustle of large cities. As the name of this type of hand implies, they are in tune with nature and enjoy working with the earth. They often prefer to work outdoors and feel hemmed in and confined when forced to work inside. They are peaceful people who take life as it comes, which means they generally lead long, happy, stress-free lives. They are happiest when in the company of friends and family.

Suitable occupations for people with earth hands include: agricultural worker, builder, cook, craftworker, dentist, doctor, driver, engineer, entrepreneur, farmer, fisherman, heavy machinery operator, laborer, lawyer, mechanic, military, physical laborer, police officer, property maintenance and repair person, psychologist, retailer, and woodworker.

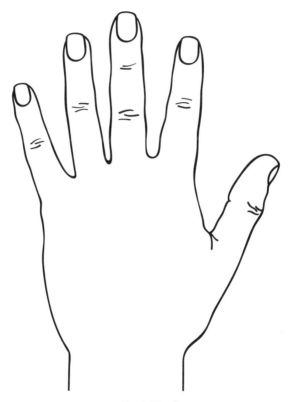

Figure 1: Earth Hand

Air Hand

The air hand has a squarish palm and long fingers. People with air hands are more intellectual than people with earth hands. They are mentally alert and enjoying learning. As well as a good intellect, they also possess a strong intuition. They are imaginative, creative, conscientious, curious, practical, and thoughtful. They are self-motivated people who thrive on challenges. They make up their minds quickly, using a combination of logic and intuition. They are good communicators, express themselves well, and make good companions. They are interested in travel, communication, and anything that is offbeat or slightly unusual.

Suitable occupations for people with air hands include: academic, accountant, actor, administrator, communications specialist, designer, engineer, IT, journalist, law, lecturer, musician, politician, public relations director, philosopher, publisher, radio, salesperson, speaker, teacher, translator, and writer.

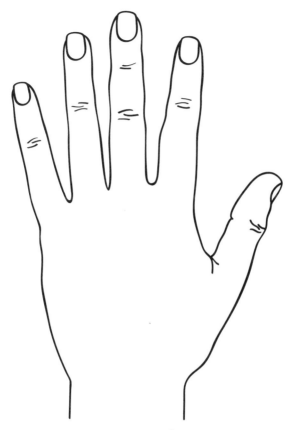

Figure 2: Air Hand

Fire Hand

The fire hand consists of an oblong palm and short fingers that are about three quarters the length of the palm. People with fire hands are creative, imaginative, enthusiastic, energetic, excitable, versatile, passionate, impulsive, and impatient. They're constantly full of ideas but need to evaluate them carefully to decide which are worth pursuing and which ones should be discarded. Because they prefer the overall view and can be impatient with details, they often lose interest before completing their tasks. They need excitement in their lives and are happiest in occupations that provide plenty of variety. They are natural leaders and dislike being told what to do. They usually enjoy participating in or watching sports.

Suitable occupations for people with fire hands include: armed forces soldier, artist, athlete, builder, business executive, dancer, designer, entertainer, entrepreneur, hairdresser, medicine, motivator, police officer, sales person, and teacher.

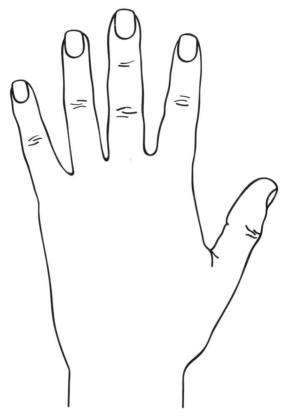

Figure 3: Fire Hand

Water Hand

The water hand consists of an oblong palm and long fingers. They look graceful and elegant and are loved by artists. However, they're not always practical in everyday life. People with water hands are sensitive, emotional, restless, flexible, loyal, and sympathetic. They're imaginative and enjoy performing creative work in attractive surroundings. They're idealistic, impressionable, romantic, and easily hurt. They avoid conflict whenever possible. They convey a sense of calmness and try to conceal any worries or nervous tension they might be experiencing. The narrower the palm is, the more introverted the person will be.

This is modified if the hand is firm and the finger joints are visible, creating "knots." This formation is known as the philosophical hand, and the person uses logic most of the time, rather than his or her feelings.

Suitable occupations for people with water hands include: actor, artist, astrologer, beautician, counsellor, dancer, fashion designer, graphic designer, hairdresser, healer, interior designer, librarian, model, musician, nurse, philosopher, photographer, poet, psychic, retail salesperson, social worker, spiritual guide, therapist, and writer.

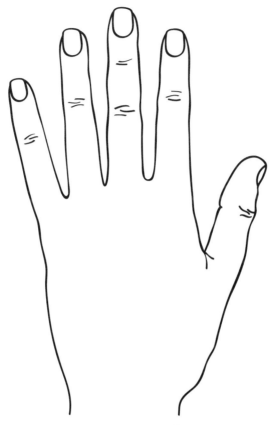

Figure 4: Water Hand

D'Arpentigny's Classification System

Captain Stanislas d'Arpentigny, the French army officer, was the first to create a system of classifying hands. He started with six types: elementary, square, spatulate, knotty, conic, and psychic. He later added a seventh type called mixed for people who didn't fit into the other categories.

Most palmists today use the earth, air, fire, and water system, but it's useful to know d'Arpentigny's hand shapes as well, as every now and again you'll find someone who fits perfectly into his system.

Elementary Hand

The elementary hand has a hard, thick, square palm with short, stiff, stubby fingers. Although people with elementary hands are good with their hands, they look clumsy and crude. The skin is coarse, and there are usually few lines on the palm. The thumb is thick and inflexible. It usually has a pronounced angle at its outside base where it joins the hand. The base of the palm is thick. People with an elementary hand work more on instinct than thought and sometimes find it hard to express themselves. However, they usually work well with their hands and have a practical, commonsense approach to everything they do. They are reliable and honest. They are also followers rather than leaders. They usually have a strong love of nature and the outdoors. Many people with elementary hands enjoy gardening, for instance.

If the fingers appear slightly long for someone with this type of hand, the person would work well in a trade, craft, or any other type of occupation that uses his or her hands.

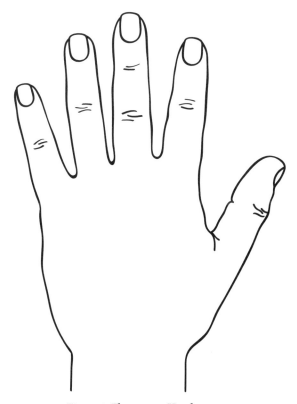

Figure 5: Elementary Hand

Suitable occupations include: building, carpentry, driving, farm-
ing, gardening, landscaping, car or machine mechanics, and
plumbing.

Square Hand

The square hand is sometimes called the practical, or useful, hand. The palm is square, with longer, better shaped fingers than elementary hands. There are more lines on the palm, too. The skin is less coarse than elementary hands.

People with square hands are patient, matter-of-fact, methodical, conscientious, determined, and honest. They lack diplomatic skills and sometimes find themselves in hot water by saying what's on their minds.

People with square hands are capable with their hands, but if their palm is slightly oblong, they'll often choose to pursue careers that are mentally stimulating.

Suitable occupations for people with square hands include: accountancy, architecture, banking, civil service, engineering, finance, law, medicine, office work, policing, teaching, and veterinary sciences.

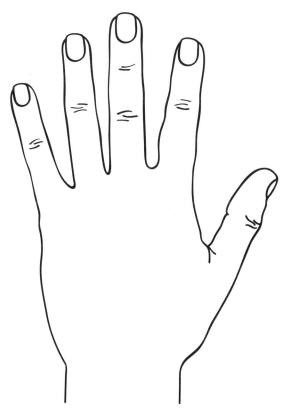

Figure 6: Square Hand

Spatulate Hand

The spatulate hand gained its name as the palm and some of the fingertips are shaped like a spatula. Consequently, the rectangular-shaped palm is broader, either at the wrist or immediately below the fingers. Spatulate fingers flare slightly at the tips.

People with spatulate hands are enthusiastic, energetic, restless, unconventional, and capable of surprising even people who know them well. In some cases, they can seem eccentric. They have inventive brains and are constantly working on ideas that have the potential to change the world, or at least improve it. They have a need to be busy and active.

Suitable occupations for people with spatulate hands include: architecture, armed forces, chemistry, craft work, engineering, politics, sales, science, teaching, and writing. Any careers that offer mental challenges are likely to appeal to people with spatulate hands.

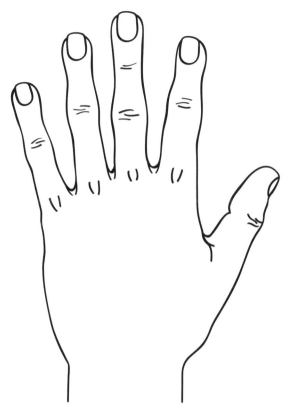

Figure 7: Spatulate Hand

Philosophical Hand

The philosophical hand is often called a knotty hand. It is called "knotty" because it has long fingers with pronounced knuckles on each of the joints. The thumb is long and knotted and often has what appears to be a waist in the second phalange (section). The palm can be oblong or square.

People with knotty hands are deep thinkers who enjoy details and like to analyze everything. They are loners who work best when left to get on with their job. Despite this need for solitude, people with knotty hands can be good company. They're cultured, knowledgeable, entertaining, and easy to get along with. They have a delightful, unusual sense of humor. They have serious interests and often become involved in educational, psychological, scientific, and spiritual matters.

Suitable occupations with people with knotty hands include: computing, mathematics, medicine, philosophy, psychology, religion, science, teaching, and technical writing.

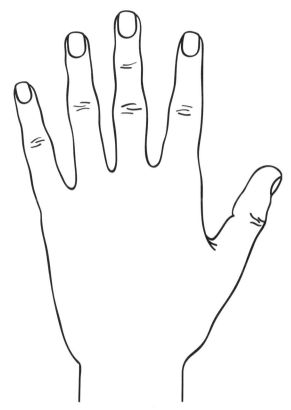

Figure 8: Philosophical Hand

Conic Hand

The conic hand has a graceful, curved appearance. The outer edge of the palm on the little finger side is usually curved. The palm is slightly oblong, and the fingers are usually medium in length with rounded, conic tips.

People with conic hands are creative, artistic, and idealistic. They get bored easily and continually seek new experiences. They often feel let down as they visualize a beautiful world where everyone gets on with everyone else and everything is perfect. They dislike vulgarity in any form. They are cheerful, positive, charming people who make an effort to get on well with others.

Suitable occupations for people with conic hands include: acting, art, business, dentistry, law, medicine, music, poetry, psychic, public speaking, reception, sales, teaching, travel, writing.

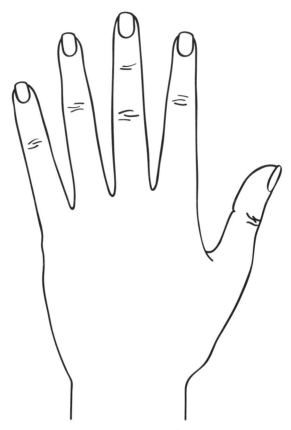

Figure 9: Conic Hand

Psychic Hand

The psychic hand is long, slender, and graceful. The fingers are slender with pointed tips. The fingernails are usually almond-shaped. The palms contain a large number of fine worry lines.

People with psychic hands are idealistic, trusting, romantic, sensitive, intuitive, and impractical. They have a spiritual nature and are often religious. People with psychic hands have a nervous disposition and worry about almost everything. They have vivid imaginations and prefer to live in a fantasy world rather than deal with all the problems and difficulties of everyday life.

Artists love psychic hands as they are beautiful to look at. Fortunately, though, you won't find many true psychic hands, as life is never straightforward and easy for them.

Suitable occupations for people with psychic hands include: acting, astrology, clairvoyancy, design, diplomacy, intuitive work, mediumship, psychic reading, writing.

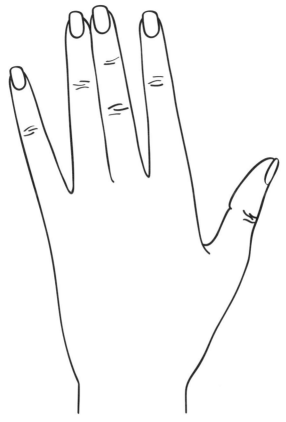

Figure 10: Psychic Hand

Mixed Hand

The mixed hand is the classification for hands that don't fit neatly into any of the other types. This can be confusing at times. What do you do, for instance, if someone has a conic-shaped palm with short, stubby fingers? How do you classify a psychic hand with a powerful thumb and firm mounts? What if the hand has two conic fingers and two that are spatulate? This classification is necessary to cover cases like these, which can be a sign of inner conflict. However, when you encounter a mixed hand in practice, the best policy is to read the features you find, rather than spend too much time trying to label the hand shape.

People with mixed hands are versatile, adaptable, positive, and willing to try anything. They enjoy change and need plenty of variety in their lives. They look forward to the future and find it easy to let go of the past.

People with mixed hands get on well with others but always look after themselves first. Consequently, they're inclined to be selfish at times.

It's impossible to list suitable occupations for people with mixed hands, as every hand is different.

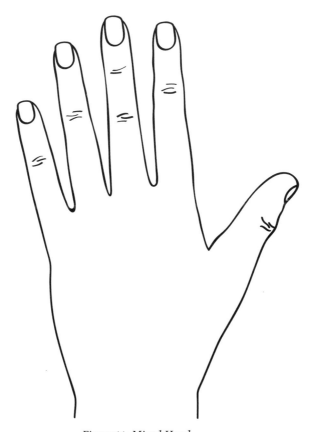

Figure 11: Mixed Hand

The Four Quadrants

The hand can be divided into four sections using two imaginary lines. The first runs down the middle of the second finger and down the palm to the wrist. This splits the hand into two halves. The half that contains the thumb relates to ambition, willpower, and actions in the world. The other half relates to imagination, intuition, and thoughts.

The second imaginary line starts halfway between the base of the fingers and the wrist. It runs across the palm, bisecting the first line in the process. It also creates two halves. The half of the hand that includes the fingers relates to activity and thinking, while the other half is receptive, instinctual, unconscious, and passive.

The two lines create what are known as the four quadrants. These are the active-outer, active-inner, passive-outer, and passive-inner. When you look at someone's palms, you'll frequently find that one of the four quadrants is more prominent or obvious than the others. Sometimes this is simply a feeling, but at other times one quadrant will be noticeably more developed than the others. If all the quadrants are equally prominent, the person will have managed to balance the different areas of his or her life.

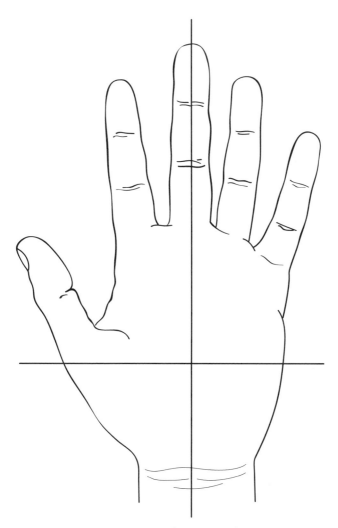

Figure 12: The Four Quadrants

Active-Outer Quadrant

The active-outer quadrant contains the top part of the thumb, as well as all of the first finger and half of the second finger. This quadrant relates to the person's desires, goals, power, and influence. If this quadrant is prominent, the person will put a great deal of energy into achieving his or her aims and goals.

Passive-Outer Quadrant

The passive-outer quadrant includes the bottom part of the thumb as well as the mound immediately below it (mount of Venus). This quadrant relates to physical stamina, the person's loved ones, and his or her sexuality. If this quadrant is well-developed, the person will possess plenty of energy and stamina along with a healthy sexual appetite. If this quadrant is less developed than the others, the person will lack enthusiasm and energy and have little interest in physical activities.

Active-Inner Quadrant

The active-inner quadrant includes the third and fourth fingers, and half of the second finger. If this quadrant is well-developed, the person will be interested in learning and the arts, enjoy a good social life, and have little interest in achieving worldly success.

Passive-Inner Quadrant

The passive-inner quadrant occupies the quarter of the palm directly opposite the thumb. This area includes the mount of Luna, which will be discussed later. This area relates to the person's creative subconscious. If this area is well developed, the person will be intuitive, sensitive, emotional, and empathetic. He or she will also be creative and possess a rich imagination.

The Three Worlds

Another way to look at the hand as a whole is to divide the fingers and palm into three sections known as the three worlds. These indicate the mental world, the practical world, and the instinctual world.

The mental world comprises the four fingers. The palm is mentally split into two halves by a horizontal line running across the palm from the base of the angle where the thumb joins the palm to create the other two worlds.

The first world (the fingers) indicates the mind and how it is used. It also relates to spirituality and sensitivity. Someone with long fingers compared to the rest of the hand will enjoy logic, thinking, and learning.

The second world (between the fingers and the horizontal line crossing the palm from the base of the thumb) represents business, family, practicality, material success, and working well with others. If this area is well developed, the person will have a social conscience and gain pleasure from of helping others.

The third world represents physical energy and vitality as well as basic, instinctive desires and urges. It relates to shrewdness and the material aspects of life. If this area is well developed, the person will put all the energy at his or her disposal into achieving goals and desires.

Often you can tell at a glance which of the three worlds the person lives in, but there will also be times when each world appears to be equally important in the person's life. This is a good sign, as it shows the person has balanced his or her mind, practicality, and instincts and will be able to make good use of all of them.

If the first and second worlds are more prominent than the third, the person will be able to use his or her logic and business acumen to do well financially. If the second and third worlds are more developed than the first, the person would also do well financially, probably in a business using machinery or manual labor.

The three worlds can also be read in the three phalanges of the fingers. The tip section or phalange relates to the first world, the middle section to the second world, and the base phalanges to the third world.

Size of the Hands

The size of the hands shows what the person wants to do with them. However, you have to bear in mind that a tall person is likely to have larger hands than someone who is short. Consequently, you need to look at the size of the hands in relation to the size of the person. As most people have average sized hands, it's a simple matter to notice hands that are unusually large or small.

Strangely, people with large hands enjoy working with anything that's small and detailed. They pay attention to detail, and work everything out carefully before making a decision. The largest hands I remember seeing belonged to an expert watchmaker who loved the intricacy of his work.

People with small hands are quick thinkers who enjoy doing things on a big scale. They are capable of handling several things at once and enjoy working on big projects.

How the Hand is Held

You can tell a great deal from the way someone shows you his or her hands. If the hand is shown with all the fingers touching, the person will be cautious, timid, distrusting, and likely to lack in confidence. If the hand is shown with the fingers spread widely apart, the person will be outgoing, enthusiastic, confident, and open. If the hand is displayed with the fingers slightly apart, the person will be a reasonably independent thinker

It's common for people to display their hands for a reading with the fingers spread. However, as the reading progresses, the fingers often slowly close. This shows that the person is concerned that you will learn too much about them by studying their palms.

As you can see, the fingers play an important role in palmistry. We'll look at the fingers in greater depth in the next chapter.

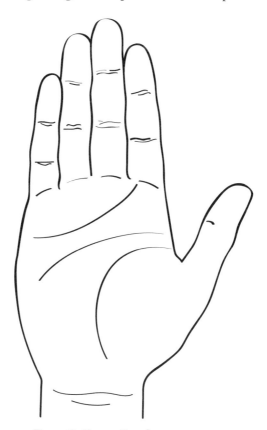

Figure 13: Fingers Together

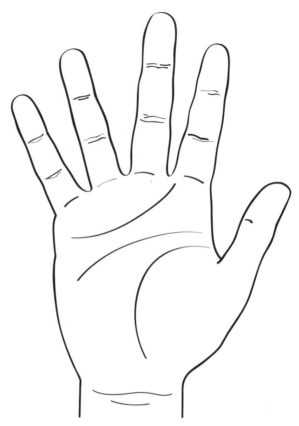

Figure 14: Fingers Apart

Chapter Two
The Fingers and Thumb

We've already learned about finger lengths and how the fingers are held when the hands are displayed. I frequently meet people who are surprised to learn that the fingers have any part to play in palm reading. In actuality, a great deal of information can be learned by examining the fingers and thumb. I usually tell these people of a palm reader I met in India who read the thumb of his clients and nothing else. I asked him why he didn't look at the rest of his clients' hands while he had the opportunity, and he replied that it wasn't necessary. I disagreed with him, and I think you will too after reading this chapter.

Gaps Between the Fingers

How people hold their hands when they don't know they're being observed reveals a great deal. The gaps between the fingers are a good example of this.

Someone with a noticeable gap between the first and second fingers, for example, is confident and has a healthy self-esteem.

This person can stand up for him or herself and is likely to build up a strong faith or philosophy of life.

A noticeable gap between the second and third fingers reveals someone who lives for the moment and has no interest or care about what tomorrow might bring. This gap is rarely found.

The most commonly found gap is between the ring and little finger. Someone with this gap is an independent thinker who prefers to make up his or her own mind rather than accept too much on trust. It can also indicate problems in expressing emotions and other deep-held feelings. This person is likely to be able to speak confidently on matters that are not important but find it hard to discuss deeply personal matters.

When the hand is held with all the fingers widely apart, the person will be independent, lighthearted, friendly, and outgoing. The fingers show this person has nothing to hide.

When all the fingers are held together the person is cautious, reserved, reticent, and takes time to make friends. He or she will be concerned about what other people might be thinking of him or her.

A small space between each of the fingers indicates someone who is open, friendly, and independent in thought and deed.

The Fingertips

Each finger provides its own special energy to the person, and the fingertip shape indicates how this energy should be used.

The tips of the fingers come in three main types: square, spatulate, or conic. Square fingertips are squarish, spatulate fingertips flare at the end and resemble a spatula, and conic fingertips are rounded. Some people have the same type of fingertip on every finger, but it's more usual for someone to have a mixture of different tips on their fingers. People with a mixture of different types of fingertips are versatile, curious, and adaptable. However, one type of fingertip will still predominate. They're likely to use the qualities of this fingertip in their careers and make use of the others in their hobbies and interests.

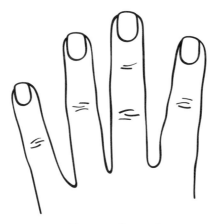

Figure 15: Square tips

People with square fingertips are down-to-earth, capable, and practical. They are cautious, conservative, conventional, orthodox, patient, and methodical. They don't like to be rushed into making a decision, preferring to take as much time as necessary to make their minds up. They enjoy details and dislike change.

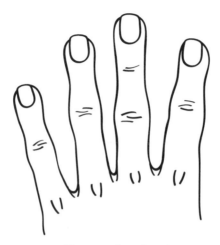

Figure 16: Spatulate tips

People with spatulate fingertips are practical, intelligent, unconventional, impulsive, original, creative, inventive, restless, intuitive, and entrepreneurial. They are busy people who seek change and variety, and love discussing and thinking about new ideas and concepts.

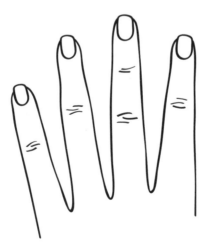

Figure 17: Conic tips

Conic fingertips are found more frequently than the other types. People with these are quick-thinking, easygoing, sociable, imaginative, sensitive, and idealistic. They appreciate beauty in all its forms, and rely on their feelings as well as cold, hard logic.

Occasionally, you'll find people with pointed fingertips. This is an extreme form of the conic fingertip. People with these are intuitive, idealistic, sensitive, inspirational, spontaneous, spiritual, dreamy, and highly-strung. They're not particularly practical and find everyday life difficult, usually preferring to live inside a close relationship. However, this doesn't necessarily make life easier, as they're possessive and have a constant need for attention.

It's sometimes difficult to determine the shapes of fingertips, and it can be helpful to run your thumb and first finger up and down the sides of the fingertip you're evaluating to help determine what type it is.

Very rarely, you'll find someone with droplets on the tip phalanges of their fingers. When the palm is held facing downward, the droplets look like tiny drops of water near the tips of the fingers. People with droplets are extremely sensitive and intuitive. They are caring, supportive, and loving. Unfortunately, they're often taken advantage of by others.

The Phalanges

The fingers are divided into three sections that are called phalanges. Each phalange relates to a different area of life. The tip, or nail, phalange relates to spirituality and intuition. People with long tip phalanges on each finger will be kind, thoughtful, and interested in the spiritual side of life.

The middle phalange relates to the person's intellect. People with long middle phalanges usually do well in their careers.

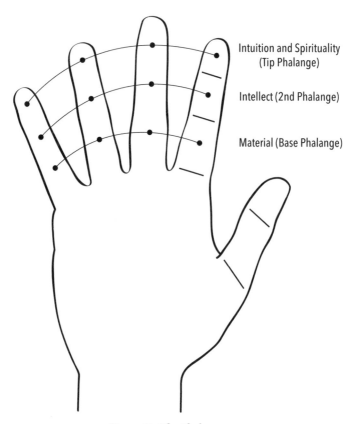

Figure 18: The Phalanges

The base phalange, nearest to the palm, relates to the material aspects of life. People with long, thick, puffy base phalanges seek physical gratification and indulge themselves whenever they can.

Base phalanges that are slightly soft and spongy to the touch reveal a person who enjoys food and is usually a good cook. A friend of mine had never cooked anything until he was widowed several years ago. Since then, he's become an excellent gourmet cook. This was no surprise to me, as he's always had slightly spongy base phalanges on his fingers.

You'll occasionally see fingers that have only one crease instead of the usual two where the joints appear. This can be found on the hands of normal people, but usually relates to a congenital condition such as Down syndrome.

Lines on the Fingers

Fine vertical lines on the base phalanges of the fingers are a sign of strain. People with these have been overdoing things and would benefit by having a day or two off. Even a good night's sleep has a positive effect on these lines.

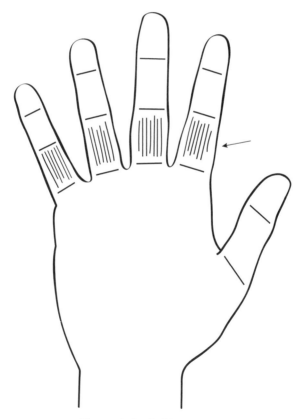

Figure 19: Strain Lines

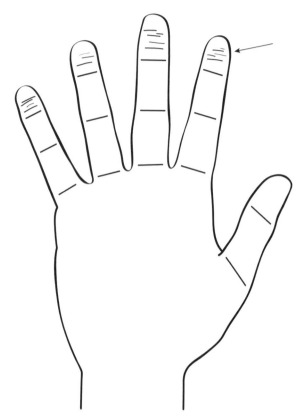

Figure 20: Stress Lines

Stress lines are much more serious than strain lines. These are fine horizontal lines on the tip phalanges of the fingers. These show that the person has been suffering stress and strain for a considerable amount of time. Stress lines take time to appear and disappear slowly once the stress-producing situation is over. The best remedy for someone with stress lines on his or her fingers is to have a relaxing vacation, or at the very least, to move away from whatever is causing the stress. This may not be easy, as these lines are most likely caused by relationship or work pressures.

If the stress is ongoing, stress lines will appear in the other phalanges. This shows that the person's health is at risk if he or she doesn't resolve the ongoing problem.

Straight, Curved, and Twisted Fingers

In palmistry, if all the fingers are straight, it shows that the person is able to make use of the qualities of each finger. Curved fingers show that the person is subconsciously underrating him or herself in the area denoted by the curved finger and is gaining strength and support from the finger it is curving toward.

A curved little finger can also indicate a medical condition, such as autism, Down syndrome, and fetal alcohol syndrome. However, a curved little finger can also be found in the hands of people in good mental and physical health and is sometimes inherited.

Occasionally, you'll see a little finger that looks twisted. It's hard to interpret this, as it may be an inherited trait. However, it could indicate someone who lies, even when it's not necessary, and is potentially dishonest. Consequently, you need to be cautious with any financial dealings you have with people exhibiting this trait.

Smooth and Knotty Fingers

Knotty fingers occur when the joints are highly visible. These people like to analyze everything they do and take little on trust. People with smooth fingers have knots that are less visible. They are more trusting and intuitive than people with knotty fingers.

An easy way to remember this is to imagine thoughts coming into the body through the fingertips. Every time a thought reaches a knotty joint, it goes around and around, analyzing and examining the thought before it can continue. As smooth-fingered people do not pause in this way to analyze their thoughts, they flow into their hands more quickly than they do with people with knotty joints.

In the nineteenth century, one of the hand classifications was called the philosophical hand. Not surprisingly, this hand contained knotty fingers.

The knots between the first and second phalanges are called the "knots of mental order." People with visible knots in this position are logical, methodical, and mentally alert. They work almost entirely on logic, rather than intuition.

The knots between the second and third phalanges are known as the "knots of material order." People with these tend to over-analyze everything and this limits their creative potential. People who have knots of material order almost always have plenty of worry lines on their palms as well.

Finger Settings

The fingers are set on the palm in one of four ways. The most usual formation is a gently curved arch. This occurs when the first and fourth fingers are set slightly below the second and third fingers. This shows that the person is well-balanced, friendly, open, and easy to get along with.

The curved arch becomes a tented arch when the first and fourth fingers are set considerably lower than the second and third fingers. This shows that the person lacks confidence and self-esteem. This person will feel inadequate and have frequent doubts about his or her own abilities.

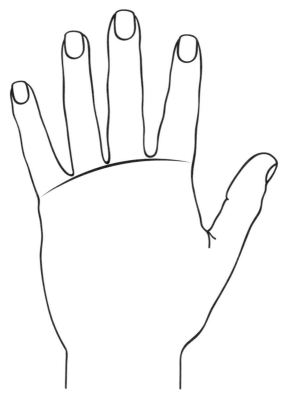

Figure 21: Curved Arch

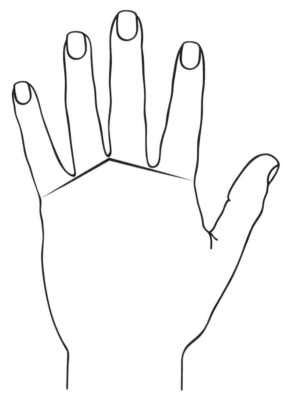

Figure 22: Tented Arch

When the fingers are set in a straight line, the person will be confident and feel proud of what he or she has accomplished. If the first and second fingers are also almost equal in length, the person will be egotistical, vain, condescending, and enjoy putting other people down.

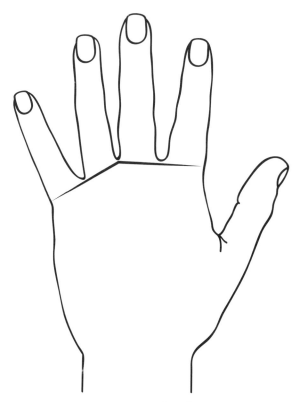

Figure 23: Dropped Little Finger

Many people have what is known as a "dropped" little finger. This occurs when the first three fingers are arranged in a gentle curve, but the little finger is set considerably lower than the others. This shows that the person will have to learn through setbacks, disappointments, and mistakes. Usually, this person's life will go well for a while, and then suddenly he or she will be dropped into a situation that takes a great deal of time and effort to resolve.

Flexibility

People with supple fingers have flexible minds. They enjoy discussing different points of view and often act on hunches and feelings. If the fingers are so flexible that they almost appear to be double-jointed, the person will be excitable and tend to dominate the conversation.

Fingers that appear hard and unyielding belong to people who are fixed and rigid in their outlook and approach to life.

Fingernails

We all subconsciously notice other people's fingernails and make judgments about them based on their appearance and condition. We assume that someone with manicured fingernails will be cultured and refined and assume the opposite when we encounter someone with dirty, broken, or uncut fingernails.

The ideal fingernail is wide and medium in length. It should be slightly longer than it is wide. Fingernails of this sort belong to people who are energetic, honest, and faithful.

Long fingernails belong to people who are sensitive, creative, and emotional.

Narrow fingernails belong to people who are narrow-minded and are unreceptive to new ideas.

People with fingernails that are long and narrow are self-centered, egotistical, and always want to get their own way.

People with short fingernails are critical, impatient, and suffer from nervous tension. They are harder on themselves than they are on others.

People with short, narrow nails that look small compared to the fingertips avoid spending money and take pleasure in being parsimonious.

Vertical ridges on the fingernails are usually a sign of nervousness but can also be caused by a deficiency in the diet.

Horizontal lines are a sign of stress or illness at the time the line first became visible.

White dots on the nails are a sign of anxiety and stress. However, they can also indicate a calcium deficiency.

The color of the nails is also revealing. The ideal nail is pinkish in color and has no spots or ridges. Red fingernails belong to people who become overexcited, agitated, or angry quickly and easily. White fingernails usually belong to people who are anemic. Yellowish fingernails indicate liver problems. Bluish fingernails are a sign of circulation problems. However, if the nails have always been bluish, the person is likely to be cold, unfriendly, and lacking in kindness.

The Jupiter/First Finger

Keywords: ambition, independence,
confidence, faith, and philosophy.

The first, or index, finger is named after the Roman god Jupiter. It symbolizes ambition, assertiveness, pride, leadership, confidence, self-esteem, and the ego. This finger will be either shorter, longer, or the same length as the ring finger (the Apollo finger) on the same hand. It's easier to determine the relative lengths of these fingers by looking at the back of the hand.

It's been known since the nineteenth century that men usually have ring fingers that are longer than their index fingers. This is believed to be caused by the amount of testosterone that the fetus is exposed to in the womb.

It's a simple matter to work out what is called your 2:4 digit ratio. (It gained this name as it's the ratio between your second and fourth fingers.) Measure your index finger from the center of the crease where it joins the palm to its tip. Measure your ring finger in the same way. Your ring finger is likely to have more than one crease. Use the crease that is closest to the palm. Divide the index finger length by the ring finger length to calculate your 2:4 digit ratio. An average rating is .95 for a man and .97 for a woman.

People with a rating that is less than average are more assertive and dominant than people with a rating that is above average. If the person's rating is higher than average, he or she will be likable and easy to get along with.

As the first finger is related to ambition, an index finger that is longer than the ring finger on a man's hand shows that he's motivated, ambitious, and prepared to work hard to achieve his goals. In extreme cases, the person may affect his health by not knowing when to stop. Sadly, graveyards are full of people who worked too hard for too long.

If the index finger is noticeably shorter than the ring finger, the person will lack confidence in his or her early life. He or she might be inclined to hold back when people with longer index fingers push forward. This ceases to be a disadvantage in later life, as the person will know when to slow down and relax and when to work hard and progress.

When the index and ring fingers are approximately equal in length, the person will be reasonably ambitious but will also take time out to rest and unwind when necessary.

The index finger is usually straight. It's a sign of weakness and low self-esteem if it curves toward the second finger. This person will feel sorry for him or herself and will need a great deal of support and encouragement from friends and family.

The phalanges, or sections, of the index finger should be approximately equal in length. If the tip phalange is the longest, the person will be interested in philosophy and spirituality and will enjoy discussing these subjects with others.

If the middle phalange is the longest, the person will possess a positive and practical approach to life. He or she will be shrewd and pick up information quickly.

If the base phalange is the longest, the person will have a strong interest in philosophy and religion. In some cases, this will be channeled into a full-time career, but more usually it's found in people who gradually build up a faith and philosophy of their own.

The base phalange of the index finger is the section that is most likely to be the longest. It can sometimes also be unusually short. When this occurs, the person will be modest, self-effacing, and happiest when left to follow his or her own interests.

The Saturn/Second Finger

Keywords: responsible, technical, reliable,
duty, conscience, and common sense.

The second finger is named after the rather gloomy Roman god Saturn, who was responsible for agriculture and the harvest. Saturn also gave his name to Saturday and saturnine. The Saturn finger relates to service, restrictions, responsibility, reality, and obligations.

The Saturn finger should be the longest finger on the hand. If it is overly long compared to the fingers on either side, the person will be a loner and need little contact with other people. If this finger is short compared to the other fingers, the person will lack all sense of responsibility. As most people have Saturn fingers that are neither long nor short, this is rare. I have met only one person who had a Saturn finger that was shorter than her Jupiter and Apollo fingers.

The second finger is the finger that is most likely to curve toward an adjacent finger. If it curves toward the first finger, it's a sign that the person is trying to gain strength from the other finger and is lacking in confidence and self-esteem. This person underrates him or herself, and may have an inferiority complex. This is especially the case if the person's first finger is shorter than his or her third finger.

If the second finger curves toward the third finger, it's a sign that the person holds him or herself back creatively and needs constant encouragement and support from others. These people are usually aware of their creative potential but often choose not to develop it to avoid the possibility of criticism, rejection, or failure.

The second finger is often held close to an adjacent finger when the hand is held open This is called a "finger cling."

It's a positive sign if the second finger almost touches the first finger, as it means the person will ultimately become influential in his or her career.

If the second finger almost touches the third finger, it's a sign that he or she is interested in the arts and would be happy working in a creative field.

The three phalanges on the second finger should be approximately equal in length. If the tip (nail) phalange is longer than the others, the person will be cautious, studious, and proud of his mental skills. He or she may feel superior to people who aren't similarly blessed. This intellect is often channeled into law, religion, or the occult. If the tip phalange is extremely long compared to the other two phalanges, the person will be gloomy, melancholic, saturnine, and lack a sense of humor.

If one phalange on the second finger is longer than the others, it's most likely to be the middle one. This shows that the person can organize him or herself, as well as others, and enjoys detailed work. He or she will be methodical and conscientious. A long middle phalange, especially if the finger is smooth and without noticeable joints, gives the person an interest in metaphysics and the occult.

Sometimes the middle phalange is noticeably short compared to the others. This shows that the person will be idle and dislike work. He or she will procrastinate and be unlikely to achieve his or her potential.

A long base phalange gives an interest in agriculture. The Saturn finger probably gained its name because of this, as Saturn was the Roman god of agriculture. People with a long base phalange enjoy being outdoors in contact with nature and make good farmers and gardeners.

The Apollo/Third Finger
Keywords: creativity, versatility,
self-expression, talent, and adaptability.

The third finger is called the Apollo finger and represents beauty, refinement, creativity, and the aesthetic sense. An average-length third finger reaches halfway up the fingernail of the second finger and is about the same length as the first finger. If the third finger is longer than this, the person will possess a creative nature and a love of beauty in all its forms. This person is likely to be versatile and talented in a number of areas, which can make it difficult to decide which one to pursue. If the third finger is extremely long and is almost the length of the second finger, the person will take unnecessary risks. This can sometimes lead to reckless gambling.

The third finger should be as straight as possible. If it curves toward the second finger, it's a sign that the person is neglecting his or her creative ability to focus on other matters, such as making a living. Sadly, creativity is not always well rewarded, and many creative people are forced to work in fields that do not appreciate this talent.

If the third finger curves toward the fourth finger, it's a sign that the person is subconsciously underrating his or her creativity. If you know a talented person who always downplays his or her creative talent, you're likely to find that he or she has a third finger that curves toward the little finger.

The three phalanges are usually about equal in length on the third finger. This shows that the person appreciates and works best in a pleasant environment and enjoys attractive objects.

If the tip phalange is longer than the other two, the person will have high ideals and will expect people close to him or her to live to those standards too. A long tip phalange usually enhances the person's creative abilities.

The middle phalange is the one that is most likely to be longest on the third finger. This shows that the person has the ability to use his or her natural good taste in his or her career. Art and antique dealers often have a long middle phalange on this finger. They find it easy to sell something they personally like but find it difficult to sell something that doesn't appeal to them.

It's rare for the base phalange to be longer than the other two. Someone with this formation will be highly materialistic and lack any interest in aesthetic or cultural activities. These people often do well financially and, when they do, surround themselves with expensive possessions to impress others.

The Mercury/Fourth Finger

Keywords: communication, curiosity,
quick thinking, and the business world.

The fourth finger is named after Mercury, the Roman messenger of the gods. Not surprisingly, the fourth finger, often known as the "pinky finger," relates to communication, as well as commerce and money.

An average-length fourth finger reaches up to the first joint on the third finger. The longer the Mercury finger is, the more intelligent the person will be, and the better he or she will be at communicating his or her thoughts and ideas. He or she is likely to be a good negotiator, and this skill can lead to business success. Conversely, people with short Mercury fingers find it hard to express themselves. If this finger is extremely short in comparison to the other fingers, the person will remain emotionally immature. This often reveals itself with difficulties in sex and relationships.

Before assessing the length of this finger, you need to observe how it is set on the palm. Many people have what is known as a "dropped" little finger, which means it is set noticeably lower on the palm than the other fingers. When this occurs, you need to mentally set the fourth finger alongside the others to see if it's short, average, or long.

People with a dropped little finger usually suffered from a lack of confidence when they were young and throughout life have to learn through experience. They're also likely to be shy and find it hard to express what they really mean or feel.

Because this finger is related to money and finance, it's important that it be straight. If it's bent or twisted, the person could be tempted into dishonesty or act unethically. This is not the case if the finger is twisted as a result of arthritis or an accident.

The three phalanges on the fourth finger are seldom equal in length. The tip phalange, governing verbal communication, is almost always the longest. This is a useful trait in people who make their livings using their voice. Examples include actors, teachers, entertainers, and salespeople.

If the tip phalange is short, the person will usually be shy and find it hard to express him or herself.

The middle phalange relates to written communication and is usually the shortest phalange on the finger. Even if they dislike writing, people with large middle phalanges express themselves well with words on paper. They'll be able to write good letters and will usually be able to express themselves better in writing than they can when using speech.

The base phalange relates to business, money, and commerce. If this section is the longest, the person will want to become financially successful and will not hesitate to bend the truth when money is involved.

The fourth finger sometimes curves toward the third finger. This creates what is known as the "finger of sacrifice" and is a sign that the person will give up his or her own ambitions to help others. It is frequently found on the hands of caregivers and healers of all sorts.

The Thumb

Keywords: logic, willpower, independence, and vitality.

The thumb reveals a great deal about the person's character, and I've met many palmists, especially in India, who devote more time to reading the thumb than to any other part of the hand.

People with large thumbs often achieve success as they're ambitious, persistent, and motivated. People with short thumbs are easygoing and take life as it comes. They can be stubborn when necessary but lack the willpower that people with larger thumbs possess.

Most thumbs are neither short nor long. An average-length thumb reaches at least halfway up the base phalange of the Jupiter finger. People with average-length thumbs are fair-minded and can stand up for themselves.

The setting of the thumb can sometimes make it hard to determine if it is long, medium, or short. If the thumb is set high up on the palm of the hand toward the fingers, the person will be outgoing, innovative, curious, and adventurous. If the thumb is set low down, close to the wrist, the person will be cautious and think before acting. Most people's thumbs are set between these two extremes.

Typically, thumbs rest at an angle of about forty-five degrees to the hand. People who hold their thumbs like this are reasonably broad-minded but conform with society's expectations. The wider the angle of the thumb, the more gregarious and generous the person will be.

People who have a small angle of the thumb focus on their immediate family at the expense of everything else. In extreme cases, these people can be petty, small-minded, and selfish.

There are two angles, or bumps, that can be found on the thumb. The angle of practicality is an angle, or bulge, found on the outside of the thumb at the bottom of the second phalange where it joins the palm. People who possess this angle are good with their hands and often choose careers that utilize this skill. The larger the angle, the more practicality the person possesses.

This angle is sometimes called the "angle of time." This doesn't necessarily mean that a person with this angle will be punctual. However, he or she will have a knack for being in the right place at the right time. This angle gives people a good sense of timing. Stand-up comedians, for example, need a good sense of timing when performing their routines.

Many people have no angle at the base of the second phalange. These people are not naturally dexterous and are better off working in occupations that use their heads more than their hands.

The second angle on the thumb is found at the base of the thumb where it joins the wrist. It is called the "angle of pitch." It gives people who possess it a good ear for music and a natural sense of rhythm.

Many entertainers have both angles on their palms. This gives them a good sense of timing, a good ear, and a natural sense of rhythm, all useful qualities for a versatile entertainer.

Like the fingers, the thumb has three phalanges. The first two are on the thumb, while the third comprises the mount, or mound, of flesh that is encircled by the life line. This area is called the "mount of Venus." We'll look at the mounts in the next chapter.

The tip phalange of the thumb relates to willpower, and the second phalange relates to logic. If these are similar in length, the person will possess an equal amount of logic and willpower. This person will think first and then act.

The most common formation is for the middle phalange to be longer than the tip phalange. People with this formation come up with good ideas but seldom get around to making them happen. They procrastinate and daydream much more than they act.

When the tip phalange is longer than the second phalange, the person will be impulsive and act before thinking the matter through. He or she will make many mistakes but will get up again after each one and keep on going. As a result of this persistence, people with this formation often achieve success.

Many people have what is known as a "waisted thumb." This occurs when the second phalange curves inward on both sides and looks as if it has a waist. People with a waisted thumb are tactful, diplomatic, and empathetic. These people are often taken advantage of, but they can also tell people where to go in such a gentle way that they don't fully realize what has been said until they think about it later.

Many people have heard of the "murderer's thumb." Over the years, several people with this formation on their hands have shown it to me, as they were worried about what it meant. The first phalange of the murderer's thumb is like a bulbous knob sitting on top of the second phalange. This shows that the person will be tolerant and understanding for a long time, but then something inconsequential will cause them to erupt in sudden anger. This is probably why this type of thumb gained such a bad name.

Interestingly, this type of thumb is usually inherited. Once I met a man with murderer's thumbs who told me his grandfather, father, and son all had similar thumbs.

Missing Fingers

Some people are born with deformed or missing fingers, while others have lost fingers in accidents. The absence of a finger can be interpreted as it indicates a lost potential. For instance, if the index finger is absent, the person will have lost some of his or her personal power and confidence. If the middle finger is missing, the person will have lost some of his or her potential to express feelings. If the ring finger is missing, the person will have lost some of his or her creative potential. If the little finger is missing, the person will have lost some of his or her ability to communicate effectively. If the thumb is missing, the person will have lost some of his potential for recognition and fame.

Naturally, the loss of any body part is a personal tragedy. However, I've met several people who've lost all or part of a finger and turned it to their advantage. One man I met told me he'd found more peace of mind after losing his index finger. He told me that he always felt driven to greater and greater success at the expense of his home and family life. After losing the finger, he became quieter, kinder, and more loving. He started putting his family ahead of his career and is a much happier person as a result.

Now that we've looked at the shape of the hand, fingers, and thumb, it's time to examine the lines and other markings on the palm. In the next chapter, we'll look at raised areas on the palm, known as the mounts.

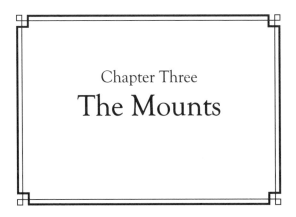

Chapter Three
The Mounts

In 1900, William Benham, an American palmist, published his book *The Laws of Scientific Hand Reading*. It was a remarkable book for its time and is still in print today. It included his system of hand classification that uses seven of the mounts (Jupiter, Saturn, Apollo, Mercury, Venus, and Luna).

Some palmists still use this system, but it has never gained great popularity as it can be difficult to determine the dominant mount in the hand. However, his system is useful whenever you look at a hand that contains an obviously prominent mount, as it provides an immediate clue to the person's personality and interests.

There are nine mounts on the palm of the hand. They are all named after planets, and the qualities associated with any particular planet relates to its specific mount.

As the mounts reveal what the person likes to do, they are useful in helping people decide on a career that they'll enjoy and do well in. The mounts also reveal how much energy the person is willing to put into different areas of his or her life.

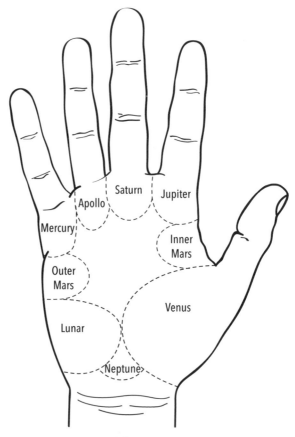

Figure 24: The Mounts

As their name indicates, the mounts are usually small raised mounds on the surface of the palm. However, this is not always the case, and mounts can also be flat or even inverted in some cases.

A well-developed, high mount shows that the person has significant potential in the area indicated by the mount. Conversely, an underdeveloped, hollow mount shows little interest or potential in that particular area. Most people's mounts are neither high nor low. This means that a normal mount is almost flat rather than raised.

The mounts can be regarded as batteries containing energy. Consequently, a large, high, firm mount contains much more energy than a mount that is flat or inverted. Because of this, large mounts reveal what the person is interested in and gets enthusiastic about. Everyone pays more attention to activities they enjoy, and naturally we put more enthusiasm and energy into those areas than we do on tasks that we have to do but don't particularly care about.

The height and quality of the mounts change to reflect what is going on in the person's life and the amount of energy he or she has available. If you examine your mounts when you're full of energy and then check them again when you're feeling really tired, there will be a noticeable difference.

You can also permanently change the size and quality of a particular mount by exercising it. If you normally avoid leadership positions, for instance, you'll be able to feel the changes in your mount of Jupiter if you take on the role of president of a club or association you belong to.

The easiest mount to see is the mount of Venus, which is the third phalange of the thumb. It contains the mound of flesh at the base of the thumb that is encircled by the life line.

There are mounts at the base of the four fingers, too. The mount of Jupiter is below the base of the index finger, for instance. The mounts below the other fingers are usually displaced slightly, making them appear between the fingers rather than directly under them. The mount of Apollo, for instance, is usually located between the base of the ring finger and the base of either the little or middle fingers.

Halfway down the side of the hand below the mount of Mercury, which is situated below the little finger, is the mount of outer Mars, and below that is the mount of Luna.

In the center of the base of the hand between the mounts of Luna and Venus is the mount of Neptune.

The final mount, known as the mount of inner Mars, is situated between the mounts of Jupiter and Venus.

Ideally, the mounts should be high and wide. The height reveals the amount of energy and enthusiasm the person is prepared to devote to the area related to the mount. The width shows how much mental effort the person is willing to put into that area.

When you start looking at mounts, you'll find it easier to locate and assess them if you hold the hand at eye level and look down the palm. Do this with as many hands as possible and you'll soon be able to check and examine them without needing to have the hand held in front of you.

There are three factors to consider when first looking at the mounts. Not every mount will be raised. Some will be flat and others may appear inverted. You'll also find many palms that don't have any prominent mounts. To complicate matters further, you'll find that most of the finger mounts are displaced. The mount of Mercury, for instance, is more likely to be found between the third and fourth fingers rather than directly below the fourth finger.

While examining the mounts, determine which one is the most prominent mount on the hand. Press on it to see how firm it is. A firm mount shows that the person is making use of the knowledge he has learned. A soft mount means that the person has gained knowledge but isn't using it to enhance his or her life.

If all the mounts appear to be equally well developed, it might be impossible to determine which mount is the most dominant. This is a sign of confidence, ability, and enthusiasm. People who have hands like this aim high and persist until they achieve their goals. Hands with well-developed mounts are called "lucky hands." This is a misnomer though, as these people are prepared to put in the hard work and persistence necessary to achieve their goals.

Many people have palms that seem to lack mounts. They are there, of course, but aren't easy to see, as the qualities of each mount have not been developed. People with hands like this achieve little as they lack confidence in their skills. If someone with this combination became motivated and worked hard to achieve a specific goal, in time the persistence and effort would be revealed in the relevant mount.

The Mount of Jupiter

Keywords: generosity, independence, leadership,
integrity, ambition, expansion, growth,
confidence, spirituality, loyalty, dignity, and justice.

The mount of Jupiter is situated on the palm of the hand immediately under the index (Jupiter) finger. A high, wide, and firm mount of Jupiter is a sign that the person is intelligent, has good self-esteem, and possesses leadership qualities. He or she will also have a jovial approach to life. (*Jove* is another name for the Roman god Jupiter.) This person will have the necessary drive and ambition to set goals and become successful.

Well-developed mounts of Jupiter are often found on the hands of charismatic leaders, such as politicians and religious leaders. The mount of Jupiter has considerable power. If this mount is strong, the other mounts usually are too.

If the mount of Jupiter is small or flat, the person will subconsciously hold him or herself back with confidence and self-esteem issues. He or she will lack ambition and confidence. This person is also likely to suffer from stress and anxiety in social situations.

It's a sign of vanity and egotism if the mount of Jupiter is high but feels soft and spongy. This person will always seek to be the center of attention and will overindulge in food and other pleasures.

The interpretation changes if a mount is displaced from its normal position. If the mount of Jupiter is displaced toward the edge of the hand instead of being directly under the index finger, the person will be egotistical and unconventional. He or she will act in an unpredictable manner.

More usually, a displaced Jupiter mount will be set toward the middle finger. This person will be studious, thoughtful, and self-conscious. He or she will also be cautious and will often think for months, or even years, before doing something major, such as changing jobs. Rarely, the mount of Jupiter will be displaced toward the thumb. This is a sign that the person will be strongly aware of his or her family heritage, and this legacy will play a major role in his or her life.

The Mount of Saturn

Keywords: saturnine, wisdom, reliability, responsibility, security, duty, endurance, conscientious, mystical, solitary, stability, melancholy, and believer in traditional values.

The mount of Saturn is located at the base of the middle finger. It is usually flat rather than raised and is almost always the least prominent mount on the hand.

People with a well-developed mount of Saturn are patient, hardworking, and enjoy spending time on their own. They find it hard to commit to a relationship and have difficulty in expressing love and affection. They enjoy work that is detailed and involved and prefer doing it on their own with little input from others. They enjoy researching and learning about involved subjects, such as philosophy, religion, and law. They like a quiet life and prefer to live away from the hustle and bustle of large cities,

Most people have a flat area under their second fingers. They're independent and enjoy the company of others but can also enjoy time on their own without feeling lonely.

Few people have a Saturn mount directly below the second finger; it's usually displaced to one side. When this mount is displaced toward the index finger, the person will gain positivity and optimism. This also occurs when this mount is displaced toward the ring finger, but people with this formation need plenty of time on their own.

The Mount of Apollo

Keywords: enthusiasm, creativity, the arts, self-expression, versatility, harmony, happiness, family, sociability, and people skills.

The mount of Apollo is always a positive mount. It's found at the base of the ring (Apollo) finger.

People with a well-developed mount of Apollo are enthusiastic, aesthetic, adaptable, and versatile. They possess good taste and enjoy working in attractive surroundings. They get along well with others and enjoy socializing and enjoying happy times with friends.

When this mount is high and wide, the person will be vain and will embellish and exaggerate the truth to try to impress others.

People who have a soft and spongy mount of Apollo are self-indulgent and insincere. They fantasize about all the wonderful things they're going to do but rarely make any effort to achieve them. Because they're charming, enthusiastic, and persuasive, they have the ability to captivate others with their ideas—at least until they realize it's nothing but idle talk.

Sometimes this mount is flat and appears to be absent. People with a flat mount of Apollo are extremely practical, but lack imagination and the aesthetic sense usually attributed to Apollo.

The creativity is enhanced if the Apollo mount is displaced toward the middle finger. This person will enjoy creating beautiful things but have no interest in being in the limelight. People with this placement get on well with young people and often choose to work in a career that involves children.

If the Apollo mount is slightly displaced toward the little finger, the person will have a talent for performing, directing, and producing. He or she will enjoy being the center of attention. This placement also shows that the person relates well to all living things. He or she may well be interested in gardening or may have a number of pets in addition to many human friends.

The Mount of Mercury

Keywords: self-expression, communication, verbal skills,
quick thinking, spontaneity, and dealing with the public.

The mount of Mercury is found at the base of the little (Mercury) finger, usually displaced slightly toward the mount of Apollo.

People with a well-developed mount of Mercury are affectionate, friendly, and easy to get along with. They are interested in what's going on in the world, as well as their local communities. They enjoy mental challenges and generally do well in the business world. They are good judges of character. These qualities are enhanced if the fourth finger is long.

If the mounts of Mercury and Apollo are well developed, the person will be a persuasive speaker and may become involved in debating or oratory.

If the mount of Mercury is undeveloped, the person will be insincere, deceptive, and unreliable. This creates communication problems in his or her relationships with others.

The mount of Mercury is frequently displaced toward the mount of Apollo. People who have this formation have a cheerful, positive, lighthearted approach to life. This makes them popular but can work against them when a more serious outlook is required.

The mount of Mercury is occasionally displaced toward the side of the hand. People who have this are brave and possess courage when placed in difficult situations.

Sometimes the Mercury and Apollo mounts appear as one large, single mount. People who have this are highly creative and work well in fields that require this. However, they usually need to be managed by others, as they have a tendency to scatter their energies over too wide an area.

The Mount of Venus

Keywords: love, sexuality, friendship, sympathy, affection,
enthusiasm, vitality, stamina, motivation, music,
and passion for life.

The mount of Venus is located at the base of the thumb and is encircled by the life line.

When the mount of Venus is reasonably high, the person will be open, affectionate, positive, and understanding. This person will be happiest inside a good relationship. He or she will have plenty of enthusiasm and energy. He or she will have a light-hearted, carefree, and happy approach to life, and this draws people to them. This person will be passionate about something that excites and inspires him or her. This can be anything but is likely to be an important hobby or interest.

A low, flat mount of Venus indicates a cold nature and a lack of energy.

This mount plays an important role in determining compatibility, as the height of the mount reveals how passionate the person is. Ideally, the two people involved in a relationship should have mounts that are similar in height. Problems are inevitable if one partner has a high mount of Venus and the other person has a low, flat, or even inverted mount.

The life line determines the width of this mount. A large mount of Venus reveals someone who is generous, considerate, and warm-hearted. A wide mount also gives enthusiasm, stamina, and energy.

When the life line hugs the thumb, creating a narrow mount of Venus, the person will be cautious, lethargic, and lack energy and zest for life.

The Mounts of Mars

Keywords: courage, bravery, persistence, assertiveness, determination, athleticism, calmness, and self-control.

There are two mounts of Mars, known as the inner and outer Mars. Inner Mars is found inside the life line between the thumb and index finger. It is the small piece of flesh that folds when the thumb moves.

The mount of inner Mars reveals how, or if, the person is able to stand up for him or herself. It shows how physically courageous the person can be. It provides aggression, too, which is usually applied to physical goals and competitions, such as sports. This mount should be firm to the touch. People with strong mounts of inner Mars often go into careers that utilize these capabilities. The police, armed forces, and fire service are good examples of possible careers. If this mount feels soft and spongy, the person will lack confidence and find it hard to stand up for him or herself.

Directly across the palm from this mount, usually situated between the head and heart lines, is the mount of outer Mars. Sometimes the head line will end on this mount, but the heart line is always below it. This mount relates to moral courage and self-discipline. When this mount is firm to the touch, the person will be able to withstand anything that comes his or her way and persevere long after everyone else has given up.

As long as one of these mounts is strong, the person will stick up for his or her friends and be able to support any strongly held beliefs.

Strong mounts of Mars are essential for anyone involved in a competitive field, as it gives them determination, persistence, energy, and a drive to succeed.

Between the two mounts of Mars, in the center of the palm, is the plain of Mars. It should be firm to the touch. An easy way to determine this is to place your fingers on the back of the person's hand while applying pressure with your thumb on the palm.

When the plain of Mars is firm, the lines that cross it (destiny, heart, and head) will be able to function well. When the plain of Mars is soft and spongy, the person will be easily influenced by others and make mistakes in choosing friends.

The Mount of Luna

Keywords: emotions, sensitivity, subconscious, creativity,
imagination, dreams, idealism, mysticism, intuition,
spirituality, and travel.

The mount of Luna is situated on the side of the hand between the mount of outer Mars and the wrist on the percussion (fourth finger) side. It represents the person's emotional nature as well as his or her imagination and creativity.

Like the other mounts, the mount of Luna should be firm to the touch. If this mount is the dominant mount on the hand, the person will have plenty of ideas and will daydream about success, but unless there are other positive indications in the hand, they will lack the energy and drive that are necessary to achieve it.

A well-developed mount of Luna enhances creativity, especially writing, as writer's forks frequently end close to, or on, this mount.

If the mount of Luna is high, the person will have a restless nature that creates a strong interest in travel.

If this mount is deficient or absent, the person will lack imagination and deal only with verifiable facts.

A strong mount of Luna often creates a distinct curve on the side of the hand. This is known as a creative curve and is often seen on the hands of people who make good use of their ideas. This creativity can come out in a variety of ways, in many different careers. Beauticians, cooks, hairdressers, and teachers of art and music are a few examples. A receptionist who ensures there's a vase of freshly-cut flowers on her desk is another.

The Mount of Neptune

Keywords: eloquence, quickness of the mind, and the connection
between the conscious and subconscious minds.

The mount of Neptune is found at the base of the hand, next to
the wrist and between the mounts of Venus and Luna. When it
is firm, it creates a level surface at the base of the hand where all
three mounts meet.

When the mount of Neptune is well-developed, the person
will enjoy speaking in public and be able to think quickly on his or
her feet. This mount is usually well-developed on the hands of entertainers, presenters, trainers, professional speakers, and anyone
else who has to speak in public.

This mount connects the mounts of Venus and Luna, which
symbolize our conscious and subconscious energies. If the three
mounts are equal in height, the person will be able to come up
with good ideas and make them a reality. This combination is also
found frequently in psychics and spiritual people who use it to con-
nect with their innate spirituality.

In recent years, the base section of the mount of Luna, nearest
the wrist, has been called the mount of Pluto. If this area is well
developed, it gives an interest in, and ability at, the occult.

In the next chapter, we'll look at the fingerprints and skin ridge
patterns.

Chapter Four
Fingerprints and Skin Ridge Patterns

The entire surface of the palm is made up of extremely fine skin ridge patterns. They are so fine that, unless you have good eyesight, you need a magnifying glass to see them. The medical profession calls these lines "epidermal ridges." The skin ridge patterns are formed when the fetus is eight or nine weeks old.

Fingerprints are the most obvious of these, and they've been used for identification purposes in the Western world for well over a hundred years. Apparently, the Chinese were the first to discover the uniqueness of fingerprints and have used them for identification purposes for hundreds of years.

In 1892, Sir Francis Galton proved that no two sets of fingerprints were exactly the same, and since then, fingerprints have been used all around the world to identify criminals. Although not even identical twins have a full set of fingerprints that are exactly the same, it is possible for someone to have one fingerprint on their hands that is almost identical to a fingerprint on the hand of a complete stranger.

The study of skin ridge patterns is called dermatoglyphics—from the ancient Greek *dermato*, for skin, and *glyph*, meaning carving. The name was coined by Dr. Harold Cummins, professor of anatomy at Tulane University in New Orleans, in 1926. The medical and scientific establishment were skeptical about his findings and it took them twenty years to accept that his research into skin ridge patterns could be used as a valuable diagnostic tool. Dermatoglyphics are now used in a variety of fields including genetics, forensic medicine, psychology, and anthropology. Not surprisingly, Dr. Cummins is considered the father of dermatoglyphics.

Over the last fifty years, the person who has had the most influence in the non-medical uses of fingerprints is Richard Unger. His method of working out your life purpose using fingerprints is explained in his book, *Lifeprints*.

Figure 24: Whorl, Loop, and Arch

There are three major types of fingerprints: loops, whorls, and arches. Around the world, loops are by far the most commonly found category of fingerprint.

Loops

People with loops in their fingerprint patterns can adjust and fit in to almost any type of situation. They are adaptable, versatile, sociable people who work well with others. They work well as part of a team. They become bored easily and need plenty of variety in their lives to be happy. They sometimes find it hard to keep their feelings under control, and this can cause problems when taken to extremes.

There are two types of loop patterns. Ulnar loops start from the little finger side of the finger and point toward the thumb side of the hand. Radial loops do the opposite, starting from the thumb side of the finger and pointing toward the little finger.

Both types of loops are versatile, adaptable, flexible, and sociable. But people with radial loops find it easier to stand up for themselves than people with ulnar loops, who are not as assertive.

A loop on the index finger reveals a charming, friendly, versatile, thoughtful, and caring person who gets on well with others but sometimes finds it hard to say no. He or she always takes into account the needs of others.

A loop on the middle finger reveals a person with no fixed views on anything. This person will change his or her mind on any topic depending on the viewpoint of the audience.

A loop on the ring finger reveals someone who has good taste and enjoys beauty in all its forms. He or she will always want to be at the forefront of any new trend and will enjoy pushing back the boundaries.

A loop on the little finger reveals someone who enjoys learning new information. This person will have excellent verbal skills and be both diplomatic and persuasive.

A loop on the thumb reveals someone who can be tactful and diplomatic, even when asserting him or herself. This person usually succeeds in getting whatever he or she wants.

Composite Loop

A composite loop is formed when two loops are entwined. This creates a more complex personality who can evaluate different points of view and assess a variety of different options at the same time.

Whorls

Whorls are concentric circles inside the fingerprints. People who have these are independent, intense, and individualistic. The whorls give originality to the qualities represented by the finger or fingers they are found on. These people are also motivated, ambitious, and hardworking. Consequently, they often achieve success in their careers. They take time in making decisions, as they like to analyze and research everything in detail and take little on trust. When used negatively, the whorl creates someone who procrastinates and finds it hard to make decisions.

It's not unusual to find one whorl on a hand. People with more than one whorl tend to be secretive and seldom confide in others. These people find it hard to delegate, as they lack trust in the ability of others to do the job.

A whorl on the index finger gives the person ambition and the drive to succeed. This person will achieve his or her goals by making the most of his or her originality and unusual ideas. Early on in life, this person will probably need to try several different types of occupation before finding the right niche for him or herself.

A whorl on the middle finger reveals someone who enjoys analyzing situations in great depth before making up his or her mind. This person prefers to make up his or her own mind with little input from others. It's almost impossible to change his or her mind once it's been made up.

A whorl on the ring finger reveals someone who is original, creative, and unorthodox. This person will sometimes deliberately shock others by expressing views he or she doesn't actually hold, purely to enjoy the reaction he or she receives. He or she would work well in an artistic field. Whorls are most commonly found on the ring finger.

A whorl on the little finger reveals someone who expresses his or her original ideas well. This person will be a good conversationalist on areas that interest him or her but will have no interest in discussing topics that don't appeal to them.

A whorl on the thumb reveals someone who is determined, stubborn, and extremely ambitious. This person will set worthwhile goals and then do whatever is necessary to achieve them.

Arches

People with arches in their fingerprints are conscientious, cautious, reliable, and loyal. They are practical people with a down-to-earth approach to life. They're persistent and are willing to work hard to achieve their goals. They are reserved and thoughtful in outlook. They can be extremely stubborn when they feel strongly about something.

An arch on the index finger reveals someone who enjoys being in a position of power and seniority. He or she will work hard for as long as necessary to achieve this goal. People with arches on both index fingers find it hard to reveal or discuss their innermost feelings.

An arch on the middle finger reveals someone who finds it hard to discuss him or herself. This reticence is particularly strong when others show interest in his or her ambitions, philosophy, or spiritual beliefs.

An arch on the ring (Apollo) finger is rare. It suppresses the sense of beauty that is associated with Apollo and replaces it with practicality in designing and creating something useful. This often reveals itself in mechanical or scientific interests.

An arch on the little finger suppresses the verbal skills provided by this finger. Consequently, people with an arch on this finger are usually quiet and secretive, especially when their finances or career is involved.

An arch on the thumb reveals someone who is sensible, practical, down-to-earth, and frequently lacking in confidence. He or she is likely to be suspicious of the motives of others and be happiest when surrounded by family and close friends.

Tented Arch

A high arch is called a "tented arch." This is an unusual type of fingerprint pattern. People with these are nervous, impulsive, enthusiastic, and highly-strung. Consequently, they tend to overreact when anything untoward occurs. They are often creative and this usually appears as a musical talent.

A tented arch on the index finger is a fortunate sign. It shows that the person will enjoy life, achieve his or her goals, and enjoy close and happy relationships with family and friends.

A tented arch on the middle finger reveals someone who is serious and idealistic. This person will enjoy spending time on his or her own. He or she will tend to ignore problems for as long as possible.

A tented arch on the ring finger reveals someone who is enthusiastic, impulsive, and emotional. He or she will constantly come up with ideas, most of which will be impractical or unrealistic. This person is likely to be creative but will need to be carefully guided to make the most of his or her potential.

A tented arch on the little finger is unusual and enhances the person's skills at speaking and writing. It also increases the person's humanitarian qualities. All of these talents are likely to be used to help others.

A tented arch on the thumb reveals someone who is sociable, genial, adaptable, and diplomatic. He or she makes friends easily and can fit into any type of situation. This person achieves his or her goals using charm and gentle persuasion.

Tri-Radii

The tri-radii (sometimes called apexes) are small triangles created by the skin ridge patterns. They usually look like a three-pointed star. Most people have four to six of these triangles on their palms.

The easiest tri-radii to find are situated on the mounts below the fingers. You can also find them on the finger prints, the mount of Luna, and sometimes on the mount of Neptune. A tri-radii on the mount of Neptune is a sign that the person has considerable psychic potential.

The tri-radii on the finger mounts should be at the top of each mount. This is why they're often called apexes, as the word "apex" means "at the top." When the apex is at the top, the potential of the particular mount is enhanced. However, the apexes are more often found lower down or even beside the mount.

The Apex of Jupiter

Ideally, the tri-radius on the mount of Jupiter is situated at the top of the mount, exactly in line with the center of the index (Jupiter) finger. This indicates someone who is honest, fair, honorable, and ethical.

More usually, this tri-radius is sited toward the middle finger. This person will be able to make practical use of the qualities of the mount of Jupiter.

If the tri-radius is situated near the thumb side of the palm, the person will have little common sense and take unnecessary risks.

If the tri-radius is situated close to the base of the index finger, the person will have an intellectual approach to life. He or she is likely to appear superior and condescending.

When the tri-radius is centrally situated but is well away from the base of the index finger, the person will live according to his or her faith or philosophy of life and have a strong desire to help others.

The Apex of Saturn

When the tri-radius is centrally situated directly below the Saturn finger, the person will be straightforward, candid, and deal fairly with others.

When the tri-radius is displaced toward the ring finger, the person will be reckless and irresponsible in money matters. He or she might be extravagant, wasteful, or take unnecessary financial risks.

I've never seen an apex of Saturn displaced toward the index finger. I assume it does occur, but it must be extremely rare.

When this tri-radius is situated close to the base of the middle finger, the person will need a great deal of space around him or her. He or she will enjoy learning for learning's sake and will have little interest in making practical use of it.

If the tri-radius is situated well away from the base of the middle finger, the person will have an interest in real estate. This could be a hobby or possibly become this person's career.

The Apex of Apollo

When this tri-radius is centrally situated, the person will appreciate beauty in all its forms and have the potential to take their talent a long way. This quality is accentuated if the apex is close to the base of the ring finger.

When the tri-radius is displaced toward the middle finger, the person will have doubts about his or her creative abilities. This placement is usually found when the ring finger curves toward the middle finger.

When the tri-radius is displaced toward the little finger, the person will have the ability to make money from his or her creativity

The Apex of Mercury

It's unusual to find the apex of Mercury centrally situated under the little finger. Someone with the apex in this position will be a natural communicator and achieve success in a career utilizing the spoken or written word.

This tri-radius is usually displaced toward the ring finger. The person's verbal skills decrease the closer the apex is to the ring finger.

Loop Patterns

In addition to the fingerprints, there are thirteen other skin ridge patterns that can be found on the hand. You'll find one or two of these loops on most hands, but it's not unusual to find people who have none. Conversely, you'll also find people who have several.

These loops and the other skin ridge patterns need to be evaluated in the context of the rest of the person's palms. I know someone who has both a loop of courage and a weak thumb. Some years ago, he successfully separated two people he saw fighting on the street. This is totally out of character to his usual mild, meek demeanor but wasn't surprising to anyone who had looked at his palms.

The Loop of Humor

The loop of humor is located between the little and ring fingers. People with this loop have a slightly unusual, offbeat sense of humor; and the larger the loop is, the greater the person's sense of humor. The absence of this loop doesn't mean the person lacks a sense of humor. However, people with it always have this decidedly "different" sense of humor. The loop of humor also indicates a strong love of animals.

The Loop of Ego

The loop of ego also starts between the little and ring fingers but heads toward the mount of Apollo. It is sometimes called the loop of vanity, as people with it have a strong sense of importance. However, they're also extremely sensitive, which means they can be easily hurt.

The Loop of Common Sense

The loop of common sense is sited between the ring and middle fingers. As its name indicates, people with this loop think carefully before acting and seldom act impulsively. This loop is sometimes called the loop of good intent, as these people have a strong sense of responsibility and always mean well. People with this loop are hard workers who enjoy being busy and active.

The Rajah Loop

The rajah loop is situated between the middle and index fingers. People with this loop are naturally charismatic and possess leadership qualities. They usually succeed in their careers and are often honored for their achievements. In traditional Indian palmistry, this loop is a sign that the person possesses royal blood.

The Loop of Courage

The loop of courage is situated on the mount of Mars between the base of the thumb and the start of the life line. People who have this loop are courageous and willing to stand up for whatever they believe in. This loop increases the positive aspects of a firm mount of Mars.

The Loop of Response

The loop of response is located on the mount of Venus between the wrist and the base of the thumb. People who possess this loop are extremely empathetic and respond instantly to the feelings of the people they happen to be with at any time. Consequently, they should mix with positive-minded people as much as they can. They also respond to their environments and work best in pleasing, cheerful surroundings. Interestingly, people with this loop also enjoy brass band music.

The Loop of Music

The loop of music is situated on the mount of Venus close to the wrist. As its name indicates, people who have this possess a great love of music and have a talent in this area as instrumentalists, composers, or singers. People with this loop can also do well as managers, agents, and promoters of musicians. Even if this talent isn't developed, music will play an important role in the lives of these people.

The Loop of Inspiration

The loop of inspiration is found on the mount of Neptune at the base of the hand. People who have this loop are highly intuitive, and creative. They're inspired by anything that moves them greatly. This can range from a stirring piece of music all the way to a kind act performed by a stranger. People with this loop are often interested in spiritual matters and philosophy. The loop of inspiration is rarely found, and people who have it have the potential to change the world. As a result, this loop is often considered to be a sign of greatness.

The Ulnar Loop

The ulnar loop is situated on the side of the palm on the mount of Luna. It needs to be at least halfway along this mount toward the wrist before the person can use it to gain unique creative ideas. These people are ruled more by their subconscious than conscious minds and consequently have an unusual approach to life.

This loop is also known as the loop of nature, as people with it have a deep love of nature and the outdoors. Gifted gardeners often have this loop on their hands.

The Loop of Memory

The loop of memory is situated in the middle of the palm close to the head line. One end indicates the mount of Jupiter and the other points toward the mount of Luna. It's usually found on or close to the end of the person's head line.

People with this loop have extremely retentive memories. In fact, the longer this loop is, the more detailed the memory will be. People with a loop of memory usually remain in contact with important people from their past, as it enables them to discuss and relive the memories they share.

The Humanitarian Loop

The humanitarian loop is rarely found. It's sited in the center of the palm, runs parallel to the destiny line, and points toward the wrist. People who possess this loop are idealistic and constantly disappointed with life in our unperfect world. On a strong hand, the humanitarian loop enables the person to use his or her abilities to make changes that have the potential to benefit everyone. On a weak hand, this loop makes the person cynical and discouraged about the state of his or her environment.

The Loop of Stringed Music

The loop of stringed music is a small oval loop on the center of the mount of Venus. Like the loop of music, this loop gives the person a strong interest in music, but as its name indicates, it's more specialized and produces a love of music created with stringed instruments. This loop is rarely found.

The Loop of Recall

The loop of recall is a small oval loop that is found in the quadrangle, the area between the head and heart lines in the center of the palm, usually between the little and ring fingers. This loop blesses its possessors with highly retentive memories and the ability to recall it whenever the knowledge is required. This talent is enhanced if the person's head line runs over this loop.

When you mention palmistry to anyone, the first thing they think of is that it's about reading the lines on the palm. We'll finally start examining these in the next chapter.

Chapter Five
The Major Lines

There are four major lines on the hand: the heart, head, life, and destiny lines. Each of these relate to different aspects of the person's life, and the interaction of all four provides a clear picture of the quality of his or her life.

The heart line has always been associated with love. It reveals the person's feelings and emotional energy.

The head line relates to mental energy and reveals how the person thinks.

The life line relates to stamina and physical energy and shows the person's passion and zest for life.

The destiny line gives the person a sense of purpose as well as the necessary motivation to achieve his or her goals and become successful.

As the lines channel energy, they should be deep, clear, and well-marked. These reveal strong, powerful energies. Conversely, shallow lines reveal a lack of energy, and the person will be lethargic and lacking in motivation.

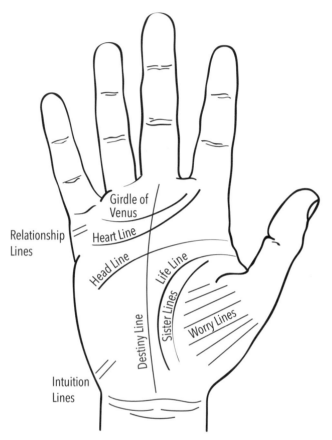

Figure 26: The Major Lines

Once you start looking at palms, you'll immediately discover that some people have few lines on their palms, while others appear to have hundreds. As most lines are caused by stress and worry, it would seem that the fewer lines someone has on his or her palms, the better. However, someone with just a few lines on his or her palms would lead a dull and uneventful life. Someone with a myriad of tiny lines would be constantly stressed and anxious. Consequently, life is more pleasant and definitely more interesting for people who have neither very few nor hundreds of lines on their palms.

It's a good idea to read the lines on the palm in a set order. Many palmists start with the life line, as it is, arguably, the most important line on the palm. I always start with the heart line, followed by the head, life, and destiny lines. The heart line tells me about the person's emotional life; the head line gives me information about the person's intellect; the life line tells me how much stamina and energy the person has; and the destiny line reveals the person's path through life. This, along with what I've already learned from an examination of the shape of the hand, enables me to build up a picture of the whole person as I read these four lines.

Heart Line

The heart line is the major line that crosses the palm closest to the fingers. It starts on the side of the palm below the Mercury (little) finger and crosses the palm, finishing close to the first or second fingers.

Heart lines can be curved or straight. Someone with a curved heart line is a romantic at heart. He or she will fall in love easily. Someone with a straight heart line will consciously or subconsciously choose a partner based on practical considerations, such as the potential partner's education, financial potential, or status in the community.

The heart line usually curves toward the fingers as it nears its end and finishes between the first two fingers, or close to the base of the first or second fingers. This type of heart line is known as a physical heart line.

People with a physical heart line have few problems in expressing their innermost desires and feelings. They express themselves confidently and assertively. Small upsets don't bother them, and even after more major events, they're able to recover quickly and carry on with their lives.

The second type of heart line crosses the palm in a reasonably straight line and does not curve toward the fingers. This is known as a mental heart line.

People with a mental heart line find it more difficult to express their innermost feelings and need to be told frequently that they're loved and cherished. They're inclined to be sensitive and easily hurt. When this happens, they usually keep quiet and suffer in silence rather than make a fuss.

From a compatibility point of view, life is easier if the people involved have similar types of heart lines that end in the same place.

The ending position of the heart line is important. If the line ends below the index finger, the person will be idealistic and have strong principles. He or she will often feel disappointed with the actions of others. This trait becomes more pronounced the closer to the edge of the palm, or the index finger, the heart line is when it finishes.

If the heart line ends under the middle finger, the person will have a lack of emotional involvement and be interested primarily in his or her own needs. He or she will be practical and realistic when it comes to matters of the heart.

The easiest ending position for the heart line is between the index and middle fingers. This provides a balance between idealism and selfishness. The person will naturally want to satisfy his or her own needs but will also be interested in the needs of others. This person will have a realistic approach to life and will keep his or her feet firmly on the ground.

You'll also find some heart lines that split into two near the end. This indicates a complex emotional nature as the person will possess some of the qualities of both the physical and mental heart lines. These people are also able to recognize and understand different points of view.

Occasionally, you'll find a heart line that splits into three near the end. This formation is called a "trident." It doesn't have a specific meaning but is considered a sign of a fortunate life. As it's on the heart line, the fortunate life occurs only if the person is inside a strong and happy relationship.

The heart line should be smooth, clear, deep, and unmarked. This shows that the person will enjoy a steady and stress-free emotional life. However, this is extremely rare, as everyone experiences their share of ups and downs in their emotional lives. These ups and downs are shown on the heart line as small ovals that are called "islands." As they usually appear in groups that look like braiding, they are sometimes called "chains." These indicate periods of emotional stress when the person was experiencing relationship difficulties.

A single island on the heart line is a sign of depression at the time indicated. Crosses and breaks on the line indicate emotional loss (heart-break) and can be a sign of separation or the death of a partner.

You'll often find a short line that runs parallel to the heart line at the very end. This is a sign that the person will not be lonely in his or her old age and will still be close to family and friends. I always point this out whenever I see it, as many people are worried about being lonely in their old age.

Head Line

The head line reveals how the person uses his or her brain.

It starts close to or touching the life line on the side of the hand between the base of the thumb and first finger and runs toward the little finger side of the palm. Like the heart line, there are two main types of head line. One crosses the palm in a reasonably straight line, and the other type curves downward toward the wrist.

A head line that crosses the palm in a reasonably straight line reveals someone who is practical, logical, down-to-earth, and rational.

A head line that curves toward the wrist reveals someone who is imaginative and creative. In fact, the greater the curve, the stronger the imagination will be. Other parts of the hand need to be looked at to determine how—or if—this creativity is being used. One person with a creative head line might compose wonderful music, write poetry, or design a beautiful building, while someone else with the same type of head line might daydream his or her life away.

The starting position of the head line is important. If the head line touches the life line at the start, the person will be cautious and think carefully before acting. The longer the two lines are connected, the more cautious the person will be.

If there is a gap between the start of the head line and the life line, the person will be independent and impulsive. The larger the gap between these two lines, the more outspoken the person will be. This becomes more noticeable the older the person becomes.

Like the other lines, the head line should be clear, deep, and well-marked. Breaks and islands on this line indicate times when the person's brain was not being utilized properly.

Breaks can be caused by a head injury, a sudden bad shock, or a mental breakdown. When the head line breaks, but is overlapped by another line, the person will have changed his or her way of thinking and experienced a major change in life as a result. A faint head line reveals anxiety and mental capacity that isn't being used.

Islands are a sign of an emotional upset that affected the person's thought processes for the period the island lasted.

The length of the head line has no bearing on how intelligent the person is. Head lines can be short or long. People with short head lines are shrewd and think quickly. They are not as interested in details as people with longer head lines. People with long head lines enjoy using their mental capacity in involved, detailed work.

Many people have a two-pronged fork at the end of their head lines. This is called a "writer's fork" and shows that the person is able to come up with good ideas and then make them practical. Writers do this, of course, and this is probably how the fork gained its name. However, all sorts of people possess a writer's fork. It means they have the ability to think of something practical, and then get busy and make creative use out of whatever it happens to be.

A pronounced bend at the end of the head line shows that the person has strong material needs and will do whatever he or she thinks is necessary to satisfy those desires.

Life Line

The life line indicates the person's physical well-being, stamina, and energy. It also reveals how enthusiastic and passionate the person is about his or her life.

Because of this, the life line clearly reveals the amount of satisfaction and pleasure the person gets out of life, making it the most important line on the hand.

The life line starts on the side of the hand between the Jupiter finger and the thumb. It moves in a semicircle around the thumb and usually ends close to the base of the palm near the wrist, encircling the mount of Venus.

Ideally, the life line should come well across the palm, as the amount of area it encircles reveals how much energy, stamina, and affection the person has at his or her disposal. Someone with a life line like this will be full of vitality and make the most of every opportunity he or she is presented with. If the life line closely hugs the thumb, the person will be lethargic, and lacking in energy and enthusiasm. He or she is likely to be reserved and introverted.

A long life line does not guarantee a long life. Neither does a short life line predict an early death. Many children have short life lines that lengthen as they grow and mature.

The starting position of the life line is important. It usually starts about halfway between the thumb and the base of the Jupiter finger. If it starts closer to the Jupiter finger than this, the person will be ambitious and motivated to achieve his or her goals. This quality increases the closer to the Jupiter finger the life line is at its start.

If the life line starts closer to the thumb than the base of the Jupiter finger, the person will possess little ambition and take life as it comes.

Like the other main lines, the life line should be deep, clear, and well-marked. This is a sign of good health and zest for life. Most people's life lines vary in strength and quality. It might be well-marked for part of its length and then become shallower and fainter for a while before regaining its strength. The time when it was shallower and fainter shows when the person's energy levels were lower than usual. The most likely cause of this is ill health.

Islands on the life line are a sign of depression or hospitalization. A chained life line indicates a series of health problems, usually caused by emotional problems.

It's common to find breaks on the life line. These can be caused by health problems but are more usually a sign that the person has changed his or her outlook on life. Almost always, breaks on the life line are covered by an overlap of the line providing protection when it's needed.

A square that straddles a break on the life line is called a "protective square" as it provides strength, support, and protection during a difficult time.

Sister Line

A sister line is a fine line on the thumb side of the life line. It's called this as it parallels the life line for part or all of its length, effectively becoming a "sister" to the life line. I like the term "sister line," and find my clients like the sound of it, too. However, this line is also called the "line of Mars."

Some people have a sister line that parallels the entire length of the life line. More usually, though, it's found at the start of the life line, providing protection during the childhood years. I especially like seeing it near the end of the life line, as this is a sign the person will be protected in his or her old age.

A sister line is always a fortunate line.

Worry Lines

Worry lines are fine lines that radiate outward across the mount of Venus toward the life line. Some people have a few of these, but others have a myriad of fine lines, showing that they constantly worry about what is going on in their lives.

Most worry lines are unimportant, but worry lines that cross the life line have the potential to affect the person's health.

Destiny Line

The destiny line gives a sense of purpose to a person's life. People with a strong destiny line usually know what they want to do with their lives. Not everyone has a destiny line. This doesn't mean they don't have a destiny. I've read the palms of a number of successful people who've done well in life without having a destiny line.

This line is sometimes called the "fate line." I prefer the term destiny line, as the word "fate" makes it sound as if everything in life is predetermined. I believe that we create our own futures by our thoughts, feelings, actions, and motivation.

A typical destiny line starts at the base of the palm close to the wrist and heads down the center of the palm toward the fingers. However, it can start anywhere near the base of the hand and finish close to any of the fingers. It usually starts close to or even inside the life line and heads toward the Saturn finger.

If the destiny line starts inside the life line, the person will be helped in his or her career by family members. Sometimes the person may feel that the help has constricted rather than helped his or her efforts to get started. The point where the destiny line leaves the life line marks the age where the person made an important step forward in his or her life. This could be a marriage, promotion, independence, or some other significant event.

If it starts halfway across the base of the palm, the person will succeed through his or her own hard work and perseverance. This person has an independent approach and likes to do everything in his or her own way.

If it starts on the mount of Luna, the person's success will come from others. In some cases, this could be friends; but if the person works in a creative field, it's more likely to be from the support of the general public. Not surprisingly, this type of destiny line is sometimes called the "popularity line."

Some people's destiny lines don't start until they're in their twenties or thirties. This shows that they didn't really know where they were going until the time when the destiny line began. Other people have destiny lines that are strong for a while but then fade or even vanish for a period before returning. This shows that the person knew what he or she was doing for a while but then went through an aimless, directionless period before finding a new purpose.

A strong destiny line is essential for success in any competitive field where you have to be clearly focused, motivated, and determined. The destiny line provides these qualities.

Palmists used to think that the presence of a long destiny line guaranteed success. However, this is not necessarily the case. Even with a good destiny line, someone who is lazy will achieve only a fraction of what he or she is capable of, as this person won't have the necessary drive for great success. I've seen beggars with long destiny lines. This tells me that they've made a lifelong career out of begging.

I've also read the hands of successful people who don't have a destiny line. People without a destiny line take life as it comes and often have plenty of variety. The ones who achieve success have been lucky enough to capitalize on a good opportunity they discovered serendipitously. Often when this occurs, a late-starting destiny line will appear to show that the person now knows where he or she is going in life.

The destiny line usually starts close to, attached to, or inside the life line. This usually indicates a close family environment where the person was taught respect for others and what was right and what was wrong. There was also support when required.

If the destiny line starts inside the life line, the person felt constrained and restricted by family obligations and probably struggled to gain a degree of independence.

It's a sign of a more independent start in life if the destiny line starts approximately halfway across the palm. There could be a number of reasons for this. It might be plenty of confidence and self-esteem. The person may not have come from a close family and was forced to stand on his or her own two feet at an early age. He or she might have been orphaned or spent time at a boarding school.

If the destiny line starts more than halfway across the palm, the person will have been strongly independent since birth. If the destiny line starts on the mount of Luna, he or she will have a strong desire for public recognition and will want to be liked and admired.

The ending position of the destiny line reveals what the person enjoys doing. Most people's destiny lines stop at or shortly beyond the heart line. As the destiny line crosses the heart line at the age of forty-nine, someone with a destiny line that finishes here will become middle-aged and set in his or her ways. If the line carries on beyond this point, the person will remain mentally active and interested in a variety of activities all the way through life.

The most usual place for the destiny line to finish is under the middle finger, or between the middle and ring fingers. People with this type of destiny line usual follow normal, conventional careers. Teaching, nursing, banking, and the civil service are good examples.

Occasionally, the destiny line finishes under the index finger. As this finger relates to pride and ambition, people with this type of destiny line are likely to follow careers in politics, philosophy, religion, or law.

If the destiny line ends under the ring finger the person will be happiest in a career that utilizes his or her creativity in some way. Art, music, literature, interior decorating, or a career dealing with beautiful objects are good examples.

The destiny line rarely crosses the palm diagonally to end under the little finger. People with this type of destiny line are happiest when they're communicating with others verbally. Entertainers and salespeople are good examples.

Some destiny lines stop, and then start again on one side of the original line. This indicates a major change of direction. Usually, this is apparent only when the person is contemplating and making the change. Once the person has started following the new direction, the two lines often join each other to form a single destiny line.

I've seen the hands of several people who had destiny lines that veered away from their normal path and touched the life line before moving on again. This shows that family obligations had to be attended to before they could continue pursuing their goals and dreams.

Squares on the destiny line are always positive and provide protection when necessary.

Double Destiny Line

Some people appear to have two destiny lines that run parallel to each other for part of their length. The second line is on the thumb side of the palm. People who have this are versatile and capable. Nowadays, many people talk about multi-tasking and how few people can actually do it. People with a double destiny line can. They may be equally as interested in their career as they are in their home life, or possibly have a hobby that is as absorbing to them as their work is. My doctor has a double destiny line and is just as devoted to his medical practice as he is to his second career as an underwater wildlife photographer.

It's rare to see a hand with only three or four major lines on it. We'll look at the minor lines in the next chapter.

Chapter Six
The Minor Lines

The major lines are the important lines on the hand and have a major influence on the person's life. Conversely, the minor lines have a lesser effect on the person's life and are read in conjunction with the major lines and the shape of the hand.

Girdle of Venus

The girdle of Venus is a fine line that is situated on the finger side of the heart line and parallels it for part of its length. When this line is present, the person's emotional sensitivities are heightened. This can create problems, as everything that happens to the person will affect him or her at an emotional level. Sometimes, people with this line will try to handle these heightened emotions by overindulging in alcohol, drugs, or sex. Some are able to channel it into some form of creativity.

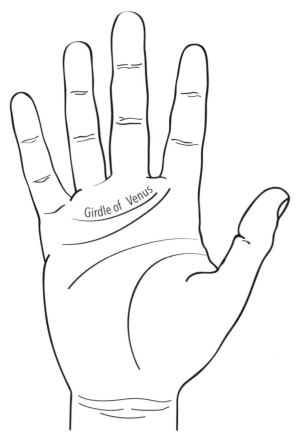

Figure 27: Girdle of Venus

Hepatica

The hepatica is also known as the health line or the line of Mercury. It runs diagonally across the palm from inside the life line near the wrist to a position close to the start of the heart line. It is never as clearly marked as the four major lines. When the hepatica virtually crosses the palm, it is sometimes considered a sign of longevity.

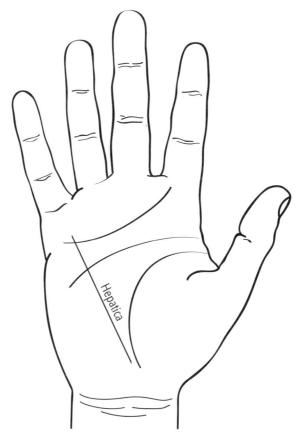

Figure 28: Hepatica

If present, the hepatica should be clear and well-marked. This is a sign of good health and shows that the person is taking care of his or her physical body. Funnily enough, people without a health line enjoy extremely good health and bounce back quickly after any illness.

Most people's hepaticas show variations in quality, and these can indicate periods of ill health. These are not necessarily major illnesses, as they can also indicate lack of energy and small ups and downs in the person's health.

Islands and chains on the health line usually indicate problems with digestion. Often small changes in the person's diet are all that's required to improve the quality of the hepatica.

Breaks in the hepatica mark periods of ill health. The hepatica should be read with the life line whenever health matters are being discussed.

Squares are extremely positive on the health line and show that the person is being protected during the period indicated.

The hepatica is sometimes called the line of Mercury, as it heads toward the little (Mercury) finger. Because of this, a strong, clear hepatica is also related to business success.

Sun Line

The Sun line runs parallel to the destiny line for part of its length and comes to an end close to the mount of Apollo. Because of this, it is sometimes called the line of Apollo. It's an extremely fortunate sign if this line parallels the destiny line for almost all of its length. However, this is unusual. It usually starts close to the head line and runs up toward the ring finger.

The presence of a Sun line is always fortuitous, as it gives the person confidence, people skills, versatility, creative ability, and the potential for success. Interestingly, it often appears on the hand only after the person has set some worthwhile goals and is working hard to achieve them.

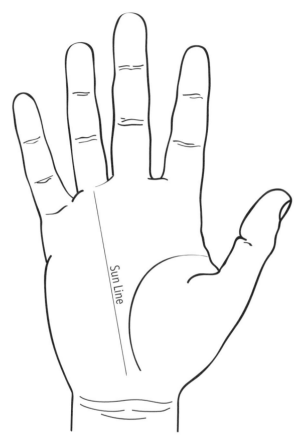

Figure 29: Sun Line

Ring of Solomon

The ring of Solomon is a semicircular line that partially or completely surrounds the mount of Jupiter. People with this line are usually intuitive and interested in the psychic world. They instinctively understand the needs of others and have a desire to serve humanity in some sort of way. People with this line often choose careers in the fields of counseling, healing, teaching, and psychology.

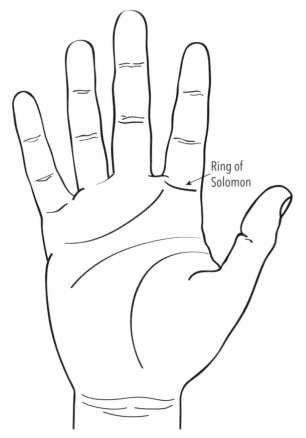

Ring of
Solomon

Figure 30: Ring of Solomon

Sympathy Line

The sympathy line is sometimes confused with the ring of Solomon as both are fine lines found immediately below the index finger. The ring of Solomon is curved, while the sympathy line is more straight. As its name suggests, people with this line are sympathetic, understanding, and enjoy helping others.

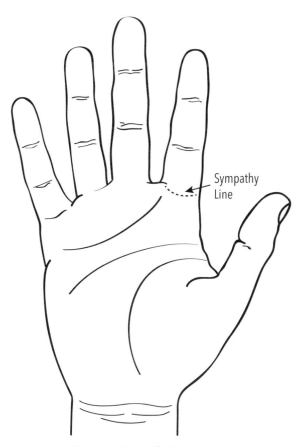

Sympathy Line

Figure 31: Sympathy Line

Approval Line

The approval line is a short line that starts between the index and middle fingers and curves onto or around the mount of Saturn. It shows that the person has good self esteem and knows how to work matters to his or her best advantage.

Ring of Saturn

The ring of Saturn is a semicircular line that surrounds the mount of Saturn. It's a negative line that hinders the person's progress through life. He or she will experience numerous obstacles and problems in both career and home life and will have to learn through mistakes and setbacks.

The Rascettes

The rascettes, often referred to as bracelets, are the lines found on the wrist immediately below the palm. Gypsies claim that each full bracelet indicates twenty-five years of life. However, as almost everyone has three bracelets, everyone would have to live to at least seventy-five for this to be true. Consequently, the rascettes are ignored by most palmists nowadays.

Although the rascettes have no role in determining length of life, palmists have known for thousands of years that when the top rascette on a woman's hand arches upward into the palm, she'll experience difficulties in childbirth. In ancient Greece, women with this sign on their hands became vestal virgins and weren't allowed to marry.

Via Lasciva

The via lasciva, or via lascivia, is a straight line situated two-thirds to three-quarters of the way down the palm from the little finger. It runs from the side of the palm and heads part of the way toward the thumb. This line is usually straight but can sometimes be curved.

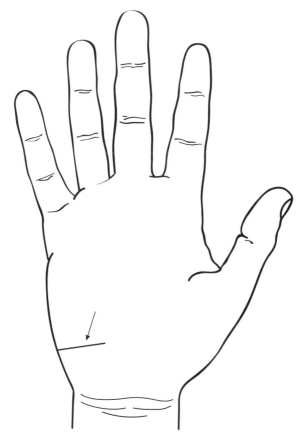

Figure 32: Via Lasciva

People with this line constantly need something exciting to look forward to. Some people with this line have addictive personalities and need to be careful with alcohol and drugs.

Medical Stigmata

The medical stigmata are a group of from three to ten tiny vertical lines that are found below the little finger or slightly offset toward the ring finger.

People with a medical stigmata are naturally empathetic and caring. It's not surprising that these lines are sometimes called "Samaritan lines" or "healing lines." People with these lines often gravitate toward careers that involve helping people, animals, or plants. Good gardeners, farmers, veterinarians, naturopaths, doctors, nurses, counsellors, teachers, and psychic consultants are all likely to have medical stigmatas on their hands.

However, many people with this quality use it in their everyday lives rather than directly in their careers. They might, for instance, be naturally good with animals, possess exceptional people skills, or be able to turn a wilderness into a beautiful garden. An elderly man I know worked in advertising for forty years and spent all his spare time volunteering for different charities. When he retired, he was able to spend all his time helping others. I wasn't surprised to find a medical stigmata on his hand.

Nurse's Lines

Nurse's lines are one or more fine vertical lines between the heart line and the fingers. They are usually found under the little or ring fingers. People with these lines have empathy and compassion for people, animals, and plants. Not surprisingly, many people with these lines take up healing as a career.

Family Chain

The family chain is a chained line at the base of the second phalange of the thumb where it joins the palm.

It is a sign that the person has strong emotional ties with his or her family when this line is heavily chained. It means the opposite if the line is thin and unchained.

This line is read from the index finger side of the thumb. It's common to see a line that is heavily chained at the start but gradually turns into a thin line. This shows that as the person grew and matured, he or she became less emotionally tied to his or her family.

A break in this line indicates a period of separation from the family.

Relationship Lines

Relationship lines, sometimes known as lines of affection, are fine lines that start on the side of the hand between the start of the heart line and the little finger. Many people call these "marriage lines," which is not correct. These lines indicate a strong relationship that may or may not become a marriage. The relationship may not necessarily be a sexual one.

A good relationship line is clear, well-marked, and comes up the side of the palm and onto the surface of the palm. This is an indication of a strong relationship that will last for a long while. A clear, well-marked line that doesn't come up and onto the surface of the palm doesn't last.

The relationship lines indicate the person's potential. Someone may have three or four relationship lines on his or her hand, but if the first one is successful and becomes permanent, the other lines will never be utilized.

It's possible for relationship lines to disappear. If you were in a strong relationship that ended badly, your subconscious mind might erase the line from your hand. However, the story of the former relationship will still be visible on your heart line.

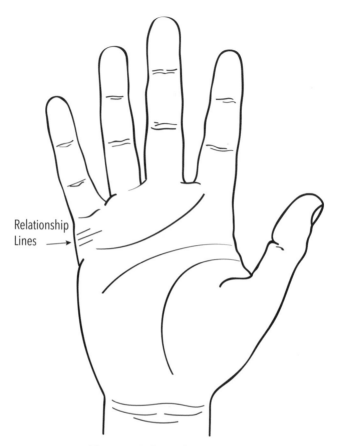

Figure 33: Relationship Lines

It's also possible for new relationship lines to appear. Many years ago, I knew a woman who had never had a serious relationship and had no relationship lines on her hands. When she finally met the right person, it didn't take long for a strong relationship line to appear.

Some palmists read these lines to gauge the strength of the person's sexuality. In this system, a strong line indicates a powerful libido, and two strong lines show that the libido is still strong in the person's old age. Weaker lines show the libido is not especially strong, and people with no lines can live happily without an active sex life.

Children Lines

Traditionally, the children lines are the fine vertical lines immediately below the little finger. They can sometimes overlap the relationship lines.

Once you start reading palms, people will frequently ask, "How many children will I have?" It might have been possible to answer that a hundred years ago, but thanks to contraceptives, people can choose when, or if, they'll have children. Many couples nowadays choose not to have children, too.

Consequently, unless I'm specifically asked about the number of children a person might have, I ignore these lines when giving a reading. Children lines can be read only as a potential on a woman's hand. A woman who might have had fifteen children if she'd been alive two hundred years ago will still show that potential but might choose to have just one—or none—in this incarnation.

The children's lines on a man's hand reveal the number of children he is close to. A man may have two children's lines on his hand, for instance, even though he has fathered three. This means he is close to two of his children but is not particularly close to the third. This is further complicated by the fact that men can become close to children they haven't fathered. When this happens, a line, or lines, indicate the closeness of the relationship. Consequently, children that are adopted, children of his partner, nieces or nephews, or any other children the man is close to may appear as children's lines on his hand.

Apollo Lines

Apollo lines are short vertical lines that reach up to the base of the Apollo finger. They're generally about half an inch in length but can be as long as two inches. Some people have up to half a dozen of these lines, while others might have one or none.

The presence of an Apollo line shows that the person appreciates all the blessings in his or her life and expresses gratitude at every opportunity. These lines are highly positive, as they show the person can keep a smile on his or her face even when going through difficult times.

Travel Lines

Travel lines are the fine lines on the side of the hand between the wrist and the heart line on the little finger side of the hand. These lines are sometimes called "restlessness lines," as they give a degree of restlessness to the person's character. Not surprisingly, this inner restlessness often leads to travel.

People with restlessness lines on their hands need plenty of variety in their lives. They get bored easily and dislike following the same routine day after day.

Clear, well-marked lines indicate important travel. However, an important trip for one person might not be viewed in the same way by someone else. For some people, a two-hundred-mile trip would be considered important if they seldom traveled away from home, and it would show up on their hands.

If someone travels regularly on business, each individual trip would not be shown on his or her hand. However, unless the person actively disliked travel, he or she would have a number of restlessness lines to indicate his or her interest in travel.

Intuition Line

The line of intuition starts on the mount of Luna on the little finger side of the hand and heads in an arc toward the center of the palm. The intuition line is usually no more than one inch long. However, when it's developed, it can extend all the way down to touch the head or destiny lines.

The presence of a line of intuition shows that the person relies on his or her hunches and feelings. If the line is well-developed, the person will be highly intuitive and would have the potential to become a clairvoyant, medium, or healer.

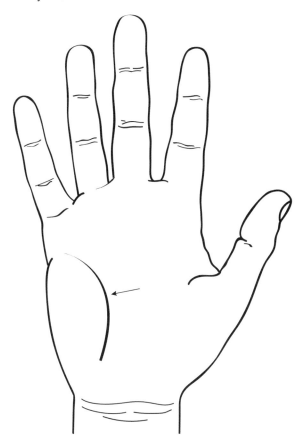

Figure 34: Intuition Line

Simian Crease

The simian crease is created when the heart and head line become a single line that runs across the palm. This means that the emotion of the heart line and logic of the head line become intertwined, making it difficult for them to express their feelings. As a result, they lead highly complex emotional lives. The simian crease (sometimes called the "simian line" or "palmar crease") is found frequently on one hand, but seldom on both.

People with a simian line are usually easy to get along with until they become stubborn and inflexible. Once their minds have been made up, it's impossible to change them. They are often exceptionally intelligent, have the ability to focus intently on whatever they're doing, and consequently learn everything they can about their work or important interests. While doing this, they're able to temporarily forget about their complicated emotions. They possess original, inventive minds that make them extremely useful in many fields of endeavor.

If the simian crease is located on the minor hand (left hand if the person is right-handed), the person will have had a protected childhood and will try to avoid responsibility.

If it's on the major hand, the person will be single-minded, hardworking, and goal-oriented. However, he or she will find it hard to relax and unwind.

If the simian line is on both hands, the person will be exceptionally rigid and stubborn. Not surprisingly, this causes major difficulties, and the person will need careful guidance and help from his or her family during the growing up years to help get this under control. This single-mindedness can be put to good use in sporting activities and in a career that requires focus and precision with little input from others.

The simian crease is often found on the hands of people with Down syndrome. However, the majority of people who have a simian crease do not have Down syndrome.

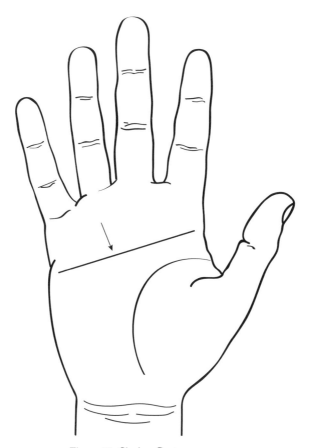

Figure 35: Simian Crease

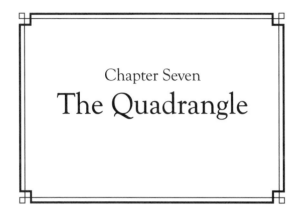

Chapter Seven
The Quadrangle

The quadrangle is the area of the palm that lies between the heart and head lines. In an average quadrangle, the two lines are between half an inch and an inch apart for most of their length and widen at each end. Naturally, this varies depending on the size of the hand.

People with average quadrangles are easy to get on with, possess a good sense of humor, and are generally upbeat and positive. If the heart and head lines gently curve, they also have a good balance between emotion and logic.

If the heart and head lines are close together for much of their length, the person will be narrow-minded, self-centered, and lack imagination and a sense of humor. There is always a degree of nervous tension in the person when his or her quadrangle is overly narrow.

When the heart and head lines are well apart, the person will be independent, sociable, and outgoing. He or she will have a strong desire to please others. The further apart the heart and head lines are, the more outgoing, spontaneous, and extroverted the person will be.

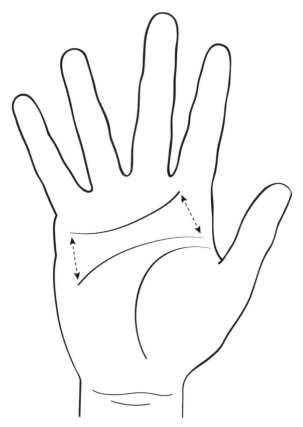

Figure 36: The Quadrangle

The area between the heart and head lines also reveals how generous the person will be. A narrow space reveals someone who is tight-fisted and miserly, while a large space indicates someone who is generous in all areas of life, not solely money.

A "waisted" quadrangle occurs when the two ends are significantly wider than the middle. As the area inside the quadrangle relates to the years from thirty-five to forty-nine, people with a "waisted" quadrangle will feel restless, unsettled, and lacking in focus and direction during this time.

It's common for the quadrangle to be noticeably wider at one end than the other. If the quadrangle is wider at the percussion side (little finger side) of the palm, the person will be honest, fair, reasonable, and easy to get on with.

If the quadrangle is narrower at the percussion side, the person will find it hard to express his or her feelings. Instead of saying what he or she feels, this person will become stubborn and rigid.

The years that the destiny line spends inside the quadrangle (from thirty-five to forty-nine) are important ones. By the time the person enters the quadrangle, he or she has developed a degree of maturity and is likely to pause at this time and reassess what he or she has achieved so far. As a result of this, many people make significant changes during this period. This is most likely to be a change of career or partner, but the changes can be in any area of the person's life.

This can also be a time when many people realize that they've yet to achieve anything worthwhile. Many of these people change their outlooks and attitudes and finally start making progress. Others simply give up, often spending the rest of their lives thinking of what might have been and blaming others for their lack of success. These people have destiny lines that end inside the quadrangle.

People who have already made good progress are likely to spend these years moving further ahead in their careers. These people are likely to have destiny lines that continue well beyond their heart lines.

The Great Triangle

The great triangle is formed by the head, life, and destiny lines. If the person doesn't have a destiny line, the third line can be formed with the hepatica (health) line.

Most people have a great triangle on their hands. If it is clearly marked and well-formed, the person will be fair-minded, sympathetic, and understanding. Ideally, this triangle should be as large as possible. People with small triangles tend to be narrow-minded and selfish.

It's a sign of timidity and weakness of character when the great triangle is faint or incomplete.

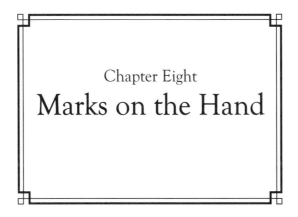

Chapter Eight
Marks on the Hand

In addition to the lines and dermatoglyphics, there are a number of other markings that can be read on the palm. These include squares, grilles, crosses, stars, and circles.

Squares

There are two types of squares. The first of these are protective squares that protect and nurture the person. Fortunately, they are more common than the restrictive squares that restrain, limit, and confine the person.

A protective square encloses a break in any line. It can appear anywhere but is found most frequently on the life line. This is a fortunate sign and gives the person the necessary persistence and strength of character to deal with potentially difficult situations. It's a sign that the person will eventually overcome the problems indicated by the line.

A restrictive square does not cover a break and is a sign of limitation or confinement. This means the person feels hemmed in and restricted by a particular situation. Consequently, the types of situations covered by a restrictive square range from someone who feels trapped in a situation all the way to someone who is confined in a prison cell.

Squares of emotional confinement are located on the mount of Venus. These squares are not attached to any line and appear when the person feels trapped in a difficult emotional situation. Fortunately, they usually disappear quickly when the difficult time comes to an end.

Teacher's Square

The teacher's square is found on, or immediately below, the mount of Jupiter. It's created by four minor lines, one of which extends beyond the square and touches the life line. The teacher's square shows that the person can explain difficult concepts in a way that others can easily understand. Consequently, someone with this square would make an extremely good teacher. Most teachers don't have a teacher's square. This is because many people take up teaching almost by accident, in the same way that people take up many other types of career.

You'll find a teacher's square in the hands of many people who have no interest in taking up teaching as a career. However, this talent will reveal itself in different ways, and they may end up in careers where they're instructing or teaching other people as part of their work. A lady I know spent forty years working in a bank. When she retired, she started teaching a Pilates class and has loved every minute of it.

Teachers often have Samaritan lines on their hands.

Grilles

Grilles are formed by several minor lines that crisscross each other. They are negative marks that are usually found on the mounts. They show that the person wastes a great deal of time thinking at cross-purposes about matters concerning his or her life. This causes frustration and confused thinking that means the person is unable to see any way out of the situation.

When found on an otherwise normal mount, the grille represses the positive aspects of the mount and often enhances the negative aspects. A grille that is situated on a mount that is flat and invisible is a sign that the person is cold and unfeeling.

Because of the number of fine lines on the mount of Venus, a grille in this position is considered normal. It enhances the natural passion of the person.

On the mount of Luna, it creates a restless, anxious person who is hard to please.

On the mount of Jupiter, it makes the person selfish, egotistical, and proud.

On the mount of Saturn, it emphasizes the person's natural saturnine qualities, making him or her morose and melancholy.

On the mount of Apollo, it increases the desire for fame but also encourages the person to waste his or her time, energy, and talent. People with a grille on this mount are often vain and conceited.

On the mount of Mercury, it creates nervousness and instability. It can also be a sign that the person will be dishonest in small ways.

Crosses

A cross formed when a minor line crosses a major line is a sign of change. The major line needs to be examined to determine if the change is positive or negative. This cross is interpreted only if it is clear and distinct.

Crosses formed by two minor lines are usually warning signs. Again, they need to be easily visible to be interpreted. A cross touching the destiny line reveals the possibility of an accident. A cross touching the life line indicates the likelihood of home and family problems. A cross touching the hepatica is a sign of a potential illness.

Fortunately, as these crosses are warning signs, the problems can be avoided by resolving the underlying reasons behind them. A change of diet, for instance, might be all that's required to eliminate the likelihood of an illness. If this is done, the cross will fade and disappear.

Crosses are not always negative, and there are four positive crosses. A cross inside the quadrangle (the area between the head and heart lines), formed by the destiny line and a minor line, is an indication of success after considerable effort. Consequently, although it's a positive sign, it can also be frustrating, as the success never happens overnight and it may take years before the person finally receives the rewards of all his or her hard work.

A mystic cross is also found between the head and heart lines. This is a cross formed by two minor lines and reveals an interest in spirituality, mysticism, and the occult. Occasionally, you'll find two or three mystic crosses inside the quadrangle. This increases the likelihood of the person becoming actively involved in the mystic arts.

A St. Andrew's cross is formed by two minor lines that form a cross that connects the life and destiny lines near the base of the hand. It's unusual to see a complete, well-formed St. Andrew's cross, but many people have a partial cross in this position. Traditionally, the St. Andrew's cross is a sign that the person will save one or more lives during his or her life. Consequently, this cross is often found on the hands of doctors, nurses, and other people associated with healing.

A cross formed by two minor lines on the mount of Jupiter shows that the person is ready to move forward in a new direction. This often involves a new partner, but it may also be related to self-awareness and spiritual growth.

Islands

Islands are small ovals inside a major line. They are never positive and are usually caused by trauma and emotional disturbances. A series of islands looks like braiding on the line. Islands are most commonly found on the heart line and relate to emotional difficulties. They indicate periods of illness when found on the life line. When found on other lines, they're a sign of hesitation, doubt, and frustration.

Triangles

Triangles are always a positive sign. They are usually found on the mounts and enhance their quality. They are often a sign that the person would do well in a creative or scientific career.

A triangle on the mount of Jupiter is a sign that the person should set high goals for him or herself. Apollo is a sign of significant creative potential. A triangle on the mount of Mercury indicates potential success in business. A triangle on the mount of

Luna enhances the qualities of the mount and is a sign of clairvoyant potential.

Stars

A star is formed when four or five minor lines cross each other.
This is a positive sign when found on one of the mounts but is
considered negative when found anywhere else. On a mount, the
star is a sign that the person has the potential to do well in the field
indicated by the particular mount. A star on the mount of Jupiter
is a sign that the person will receive public recognition for his or
her accomplishments.

On the mount of Saturn, a star indicates a fulfilling and satisfying career.

On the mount of Apollo, a star indicates the possibility of fame
in an artistic field.

On the mount of Mercury, a star reveals the potential for great
success using the person's verbal skills. This can also indicate success in a branch of science.

Circle

Only rarely will you find a perfectly-formed circle on the palm
of the hand. It's considered an indication of great success when
found on the mount of Apollo, but is considered to be a sign of
weakness when found anywhere else.

Dots and Spots

Dots and spots are interpreted only when they form an indenta-
tion in the palm. They're a sign of blocked energy when they're
found on a major line.

On the life line, this is likely to indicate a physical illness.

On the heart line, it's a sign of emotional trauma. (However, a white dot on the heart line indicates a strong, loving relationship achieved after considerable effort.)

On the head line, dots and spots indicate a period of low spirits and possible depression.

On the destiny lines, it indicates a time when the person paused and reevaluated his or her career up to that point.

Once you start reading palms, people will want to know when certain events will occur. We'll look at how to time events in the next chapter.

Chapter Nine
Timing on the Hand

Even though periods of time can be measured on all four of the major lines, it isn't easy to place specific events in time using nothing but the palms of the hand. Over the years, I've experimented with a variety of methods and have yet to find one that worked well all the time. Many palmists use astrology and numerology to help them in matters of timing.

It's possible to locate an important event that happened to the person you're reading for, and then look backward and forward from this date. You should do this with both hands.

This will give you some indication of when a specific future event will occur. Your accuracy will improve if you also use your intuition. It's possible to become a good palm reader without using any intuition at all, but to become an exceptional palm reader, you need to trust and act upon your hunches and feelings.

Destiny Line

Many palmists do most of their timing from the destiny line, and this isn't surprising as it's a quick and easy way to date important events.

The first thirty-five years of the person's life are shown from the start of the line to where it reaches the head line. It takes another fourteen years for the destiny line to reach the heart line, by which time the person is forty-nine. The rest of the person's life is taken up with whatever part of the destiny line remains. The first thirty-five years can be split into thirds, indicating the approximate ages of twelve and twenty-four. The period between the head and heart lines can also be divided into two, to indicate the age of forty-two.

There is a reason why what is usually the longest part of the destiny line covers thirty-five years. This is because this includes the growing up years, early adulthood, and working out what the person wants to do with his or her life. By the time they reach thirty-five, most people have a reasonably clear idea of where they're going and what they want to do.

The ages from thirty-five to forty-nine are usually stable years. The person will often be inside an ongoing relationship and be progressing in his or her career. If this isn't the case, any changes in the person's life at this point will be clearly shown between the head and heart lines on the destiny line.

It may seem strange that many people's destiny lines stop at about the comparatively early age of forty-nine. It doesn't mean that their destiny has come to a sudden stop. All it means is that these people have become set in their ways and consequently there's unlikely to be any major changes of direction in their fifties, sixties, and beyond.

People with a destiny line that continues well beyond their heart lines will experience many different activities in later life. Sometimes this is a sign of a late starter. It can also be a sign of longevity.

Life Line

The life line is the line that's used most often when events are being predicted.

The life line is divided in two by using an imaginary line that runs from the middle of the Saturn finger and down the palm to where it reaches the life line. This indicates the approximate age of thirty-five. You can also do this process to determine two other ages. An imaginary line running down the middle of the Jupiter finger and onto the palm reaches the life line at the age of ten. A third imaginary line running from between the Jupiter and Saturn fingers reaches the life line at the age of twenty.

The approximate age of seventy occurs when the life line starts to curve back around the thumb at the base of the hand. Once you know the approximate positions of the ages thirty-five and seventy, you can divide the period indicated by two to determine the age of fifty-two. Dividing it by three gives you almost forty-seven and fifty-nine. You can continue dividing almost indefinitely to determine specific dates.

The most accurate way to do this is to take a palm print of the hand and then use mathematical dividers to determine the years you're interested in.

Traditionally, the entire length of the heart line was said to indicate eighty-four years, and people considered themselves fortunate to reach "threescore and twenty." Many people are living much longer today, and this needs to be taken into consideration when determining time from the life line.

It's also important to remember that the life line measures periods of time, and the presence of a long life line does not necessarily indicate that the person will live to a ripe old age.

You now know the basics of palmistry. In the next chapter, we're going to begin using that information to determine people's talents and capabilities.

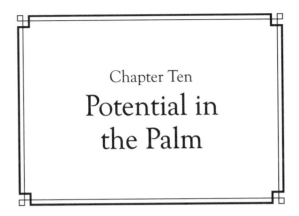

Chapter Ten
Potential in
the Palm

Everyone is talented. In fact, we all have many skills that can be harnessed and used to benefit ourselves and others. Every palm provides information that can help people find out which of their talents and interests would be the most fulfilling and enjoyable for them as a full-time career or as a spare-time interest.

Many people have no idea what they should be doing with their lives, even though a particular skill they possess may be blindingly obvious to everyone who knows them.

Even people who know they have a talent in a certain area may choose not to pursue it. They might be influenced by others to do something "sensible," rather than chase a dream. They may lack the necessary confidence or motivation to do whatever is necessary to achieve this dream. They might be struggling to make ends meet and have no time to work on developing their talent.

The first time I saw someone turn his back on a dream was in high school. A boy a few years older than me had an amazing baritone voice and was seriously considering an operatic career. He had the ability, intelligence, and drive to pursue his dream. However, his parents were concerned that he might spend his life struggling to gain a foothold in a highly competitive field and urged him to be sensible and do something realistic. When he left school, he went to university and became an accountant.

I had the same dentist for more than thirty years. He hated being a dentist and longed to be a photographer. However, he was never brave enough to give up the money and lifestyle that dentistry gave him. Each time I visited him, I commented on the beautiful examples of his work he had on display. He always replied, "one day," but sadly that day never happened.

Joseph Campbell, the famous mythologist and philosopher, said "follow your bliss." These inspirational words tell us that to lead a joyful, fulfilling, successful life, we must find our bliss and pursue it with all the energy and passion we can. It takes considerable inner strength and courage to do this, which is why so many people give up and lead lives of what Henry David Thoreau called "quiet desperation."

Often, our beliefs hold us back. When I was at high school, a teacher told me I was hopeless at languages. I believed him and didn't try to learn a second language until more than thirty years later. Much to my surprise, I discovered I was good at learning languages after all. I'd believed what the teacher had told me, and for many years his words were part of my belief system. Are you being held back by beliefs that were formed when you were a child? They have no relevance now and should play no part in your life. You owe it to yourself to let go of these limiting beliefs. As every motivational speaker says: You can achieve anything you want as long as you believe you can.

I've read the hands of many people who are doing jobs they're not suited for. Usually, these people are well aware that they're in the wrong job. However, if there are limited opportunities where you live, you might have to seize any job that's available. In that situation, any job is better than no job. I sold printing machinery for a while as I had three children and a large mortgage. I was totally unsuited to this type of work, but it enabled my family to get through a difficult time.

Of course, to achieve any satisfaction and pleasure from our working lives, we need to ultimately find a position that fits our personalities, uses our natural skills, and provides opportunities to develop them further if we wish.

Everyone is Creative

It's amazing how many people claim that they're not creative. They're probably comparing themselves to the great geniuses of history. Michelangelo, William Shakespeare, Mozart, and Rembrandt are all examples of highly creative geniuses, and we shouldn't compare ourselves to them. In fact, we shouldn't compare ourselves to anyone else.

A retired neighbor of mine spends his days making wooden toys that are sold to raise funds for various charities. He's not a genius, but he's a good, kind man who produces beautiful work, and I consider him extremely creative.

In actuality, we're all creative all the time. Whenever we have a thought, we create something that didn't exist a few moments earlier.

Many people claim that they have no talents. This is because they associate talent with the ability to draw or paint, compose, write, sing, dance, perform, or hit a home run. They're forgetting that talent applies to every part of life. You probably know someone who can use his or her hands to fix anything. Have you ever had a teacher who seemed to speak directly to you? A few nights ago, I was served by a waitress who instinctively knew what we wanted before we said a word. I know several women who have a talent for accessorizing their clothes. Many years ago, I worked for a man who had a natural gift for putting people at ease. My daughter loves baking cakes. My accountant loves his work and told me that he'd wanted to be an accountant since he was ten years old. A friend of mine makes his living as a stiltwalker, juggler, and clown. He's turned a hobby into a successful business. I know a gardener who adores his work and loses all sense of time whenever he's working in a garden.

These are all talents. The good thing is that everyone has many talents similar to these. Fortunately, even if you don't know what they are yet, they're revealed in your hands.

What Are Your Talents

The mounts are one of the most useful ways to assess people's talents, as they reveal what they enjoy doing. Examine each of your mounts for size and height. Feel them for firmness. In addition to this, feel the area on your palm immediately below each finger as mounts can be displaced or may be flat and not visible.

If the mount of Jupiter is the most prominent mount in your hand, you'll have a talent for leadership and the potential to do well in any field that appeals to you. This could well be politics, religion, or law. You'd do well in any career that utilized your skills at supervising others. You could make a difference in your local community, city, country, or even achieve something on a global scale. You're likely to be well educated and could use your academic qualifications to help you progress in a field that makes use of them.

If the mount of Saturn is the most prominent mount in your hand, you'll have the potential to do valuable work in an involved field, such as research. You'll need plenty of time on your own to think, study, and evaluate anything that interests you. Science, mathematics, inventing, and horticulture are a few possibilities. You have the potential to do well in your own business.

If the mount of Apollo is the most prominent mount in your hand, you might choose to develop your significant creative talents and turn them into a career. Your open, friendly approach and ability to get on well with others will help you at every stage. Art, writing, and acting are three creative possibilities, but so are medicine, dentistry, or any other field that is worthy of your intellect and utilizes your skills at dealing with others.

If the mount of Mercury is the most prominent mount in your hand, you'll have a talent at communication. Even if you don't take up a career in communication, such as announcing, speaking, teaching, or writing, you'll use it in whatever work you choose to do. You could be extremely successful in business. A good mount of Mercury is essential for any degree of success in life, as it provides initiative, energy, motivation, and the ability to recognize good opportunities.

If the mount of Venus is the most prominent mount in your hand, you'll have a talent for homemaking, raising a family, and music. You'll also be a gifted decorator and will use this in your own home but could choose to turn this talent into a career.

If the inner mount of Mars is the most prominent mount in your hand, you'll have a talent for helping others. This might lead you into a career that requires both physical and mental effort. The armed forces, police, and firefighting are examples. You might use this talent in other ways, such as teaching, medicine, probation, or security work.

If the outer mount of Mars is the most prominent mount in your hand, you'll be self-disciplined and able to deal with whatever life hands you with equanimity and self-control. You are physically well-coordinated and have significant sporting potential.

If the mount of Luna is the most prominent mount in your hand, you'll possess creative potential that is likely to reveal itself through acting or writing. You're interested in travel and working in this field could satisfy your restless nature. Many people with a strong mount of Luna become interested in collecting fine objects that appeal to them. Some manage to turn this interest into a career.

If the mount of Neptune is the most prominent mount in your hand, you'll be a good communicator and enjoy working in the public eye. You could utilize this talent by forging a career as an entertainer, presenter, auctioneer, or professional speaker.

If the mounts fail to reveal any major talents, look at your fingers and the major lines on your hands, paying particular attention to your Jupiter, Apollo, and Mercury fingers and your head and destiny lines.

If you're still having difficulty, you can ask yourself a few simple questions to help you discover some of your talents:

What do you enjoy doing? A school friend of mine has a wonderful sense of humor and a gift for creating jokes and funny lines. He loves making people laugh but didn't consider this ability to be a talent until a professional comedian asked him to write a script for him. He's now making a good living as a comedy writer.

What are you good at? You might be talented at woodworking, playing a musical instrument, or motivating others. You might be good with animals or be a wonderful cook or flower arranger. You might be patient, caring, and supportive. I know a personal trainer who used to be a banker. He disliked banking but loved working out in the gym. He discovered that he was good at teaching others how to get into shape and ultimately turned it into a career.

Can you turn your hobby into a career? You might spend your spare time scuba diving, cake decorating, unicycle riding, stamp collecting, making origami, playing the guitar, or doing something else. With some lateral thinking, you might be able to turn your hobby into a full-time or part-time career.

What are your current skills? A friend of one of my sons used to work in the finance industry. He made a list of his skills and abilities and decided he was good at financial planning, risk management, and networking. However, he wanted to get out of the corporate world. One day, a friend complimented him on the beautiful garden he had and he realized he had a skill for landscape design. He's now making a living as a landscape gardener. He's making less money than he did in the financial world, but is happier than he's ever been.

What successes have you had in the past? If you think back over the high points of your life, you might discover something that you did then that revealed a talent you're not utilizing. One woman I met told me that she became a wedding photographer after being made redundant at her middle-management position. As she couldn't find another position, she decided to work for herself. Many years before, she'd taken the photographs at her brother's wedding and was pleasantly surprised when people told her how good they were. Remembering how much she'd enjoyed the experience, she decided to become a professional wedding photographer. Success didn't come overnight, but she's now making a good living doing something she loves.

Ask several people who know you well to tell you what they think you're good at. Ask them one at a time, rather than in a group. Most people tend to underrate themselves, and it can be useful to learn what other people think our abilities are.

Is there anything you'd love to do? What's on your bucket list? I know a group of operatic singers who couldn't get enough work to make a living out of their passion. They wanted to travel and sing. They started performing daytime concerts for retired people. They gradually added costumes and comedy, and now they travel extensively, entertaining people everywhere they go. They haven't made a fortune, but they're seeing the world and doing what they love to do.

Another way to discover a talent is to listen to the critic that lives inside our heads. Our inner critic constantly bombards us with negative self-talk, such as: "I'm too old [or too young] to do that," "What will people think?," "I'm not good enough," "What if I fail?," "I'll never make any money doing that," and so on. We're all our own worst enemies, and we frequently defeat ourselves before we've even started. Fear, doubt, and worry constantly try to hold us back. Whenever you experience thoughts like these, it's a sign to look for the talent that you're frightened of using. I used to work as an entertainer and know a surprising number of entertainers who had to conquer self-doubt, stage fright, family opposition, and other problems before they could release their talents.

Creative Talents

Everyone is creative. I used to know a lady who arranged the flowers at the church she attended. No matter what time of year it was, she was able to use whatever flowers were available and make a beautiful display. While a friend of mine was recuperating from a serious illness, he discovered he had a hitherto unknown talent at sculpting. My wife and I know someone who has a talent for preparing homes for sale. When necessary, she replaces or rearranges the homeowner's furniture, wall hangings, and anything else, to make sure the home is at its best when it's put on the market. We regularly buy jams and pickles from a lady who spends her weeks making them before selling them at a farmer's market. These people are all using their creativity.

As creativity makes itself present in so many different ways, it's impossible to list all the traits that creative people possess. Naturally creative people are likely to have a number of these indications on their hands:

- A long ring finger
- A whorl fingerprint on the ring finger
- Conic fingertips
- Smooth fingers
- A loop of inspiration
- A water hand
- A girdle of Venus
- A well-developed mount of Venus
- A well-developed mount of Lunar
- A whorl on the mount of Luna
- A well-developed mount of Apollo
- A star on the mount of Apollo
- A strong Sun line
- A creative curve on the percussion side of the hand
- A head line that curves toward the mount of Luna
- A writer's fork on the head line
- Silky skin

Artistic Ability

The ring finger provides the first clue about someone's ability to paint and draw. The tip phalange should be the longest phalange, and ideally it should be broad. If the second phalange is also long, the person will have a good sense of color and instinctively know how to use it. There should be a whorl on the ring finger.

An artist needs a good imagination and consequently needs a head line that heads toward the mount of Lunar. This mount should be firm and prominent. A creative curve should also be present.

A sculptor is likely to have angles of practicality and pitch, spatulate fingers, a good ring finger, and a broad, square palm.

Acting Ability

Smooth, tapering fingers with conic or pointed tips are useful for female actors. Conic tips are useful for male actors, too, and pronounced joints are useful for character actors. A good tip on the little finger helps actors express themselves well. The mount of Luna should be strong, to provide the necessary imagination for the actor to "live" the role. A head line that curves toward the mount of Luna is useful, too. A wide angle created when the thumb is extended enables actors to adapt to any type of role. A wide palm provides the necessary confidence to be able to stand up and perform in front of others. Strong mounts of Luna and Mercury are useful for actors playing comic roles. A spatulate tip on a strong ring finger enables the person to express themselves dramatically. A girdle of Venus provides sensitivity and emotion that the actor can bring to his or her role. A flexible hand reveals adaptability.

Writing Ability

The little finger should reach the top phalange of the ring finger. The little finger should also have a prominent middle phalange. The mount of Mercury should be firm. The head line should contain a writer's fork. If the writer specializes in fiction, the head line should curve toward the mount of Luna to enable him or her to channel the imagination provided by the mount. A good mount of Luna is useful for writers of fiction. Knotty joints are helpful for journalists and nonfiction writers. An angle of pitch is useful for poets, as it gives a strong sense of rhythm. Short fingernails and a strong Jupiter finger are useful for literary critics.

Musical Ability

Musical ability is revealed in various ways. A good singing voice is revealed by round, spherical fingers, an angle of practicality, an angle of pitch at the base of the thumb, and a wide palm. A well-developed mount of Venus and a long ring finger on flexible hands provide a deep love of music. A good-sized mount of Luna is useful for harmony. A loop of music, loop of stringed music, or the loop of response are helpful, too. A good-length ring finger and a strong mount of Apollo are essential for long-term success in this field.

Players of musical instruments need the angles of practicality and pitch, as well as strong mounts of Venus and Luna. Musicians who play stringed instruments usually have air or water hands. Players of percussion instruments usually have earth hands with broad fingertips.

Dancing Ability

Dancers need angles of practicality and pitch as they need to respond to rhythm and time. They need a wide life line to provide energy and stamina. The mounts of Venus and Luna need to be strong to enable the dancer to lose him or herself in the dance.

A jazz dancer is likely to have pointed or conic fingertips to provide inspiration and the ability to improvise.

Athletic Ability

In his book, *The Finger Ratio*, Professor John Manning, formerly Professor of Psychology at the University of Central Lancashire in the UK, hypothesized that males who are exceptionally good at sports received more testosterone in the womb than men who are not. This is indicated by the comparative lengths of the index and ring fingers. Exceptional athletes, both male and female, have index fingers that are shorter than their ring fingers. They have more strength and can run faster than athletes with index fingers that are longer than their ring fingers. A number of tests have confirmed these findings. One example is of a two-mile race near Manchester, UK, involving fifty-seven athletes. The first three runners to finish all had ring fingers that were longer than their index fingers, and two of the last three to finish had index fingers that were longer than their ring fingers (Manning, 99).

One of the reasons for their success is that they're highly disciplined and train regularly. They also put huge amounts of energy and passion into everything they do. It is this incredible motivation and drive that enables them to be so successful.

This theory is still controversial. However, many world-class athletes, including Usain Bolt, the Jamaican sprinter, have ring fingers that are longer than their index fingers.

On a 2005 BBC television program called *Secrets of the Sexes*, Dr. Manning was shown photocopies of the hands of six competitors in a race that had not yet taken place. Based on the digit ratio of the runners' index and ring fingers he made a prediction of the finishing position of each runner. He successfully predicted the finishing position of four out of the six runners. He transposed the positions of the runners who came third and fourth. Dr. Manning said: "We've got four out of six right, but the two that are wrong were kind of quite close." (https://www.nextnature.net/2010/06/reading-the-body-finger-length-ratio-predicts-athletic-ability/.) This experiment can be seen on https://www.youtube.com/watch?v=ecd43CQo7xU.

Athletes usually have earth or air hands, as the palm needs to be broad. The life line should sweep well across the palm to provide the necessary energy for success. A double life line for part of the life line's length is useful too. A strong destiny line provides the necessary motivation to succeed. Some athletes have spatulate fingers as this provides energy and a need to act, rather than stand still.

Spiritual Potential

The mounts of Jupiter, Venus, and Luna are well-developed. A long, straight little finger with a conic or pointed tip is useful. The tip phalange of this finger should be long to provide eloquence. A conic tip on a strong index finger reveals the potential for strong religious ideals. The fingers should be long and straight.

There are three major indicators of spiritual potential that can be seen in the palm. A mystic cross, or crosses, made up of two minor lines inside the quadrangle, shows that the person is interested in the spiritual side of his or her life.

The ring of Solomon shows that the person is interested in developing his or her spirituality and has a desire to serve humanity in some sort of way. The ring of Solomon will grow and become stronger as the person works on developing this side of his or her nature.

The presence of a St. Andrew's cross is a sign that the person will have a strong desire to serve and help others. In some cases, he or she may put the needs of others first and only think of him or herself once those needs have been satisfied.

Your Hand and Your Career

According to a 2017 Gallup State of the Workplace study, only 33 percent of US employees enjoy going to work. In the same study, 51 percent were not engaged in their work and, 16 percent were "actively disengaged," meaning they disliked or even hated their jobs (https://csistars.com/2017/03/23/5-gallup-insights-need-know/). The world would be a much happier place if the almost 70 percent of people who aren't happy in their work found jobs that utilized their skills, knowledge, and interests.

One hundred years ago, palmists started suggesting that reading the hands of children was a good way to determine their natural talents and could be used to help people choose satisfying and rewarding careers. The first palmists to publish anything on the subject were Katharine St. Hill in England and William G. Benham in the United States.

Katherine St. Hill published her first book on palmistry in 1889, and as a direct result of that, she founded the Cheirological Society of Great Britain in the same year. She included a chapter on the qualities necessary for a variety of occupations in *The Book of the Hand*, which was published in 1927.

Across the Atlantic, William G. Benham also became interested in helping people find suitable careers for themselves by analyzing their palms. After his book, *The Laws of Scientific Hand Reading*, was published in 1900, William Benham was approached by Dr. Canfield, President of Ohio State University, who asked him if the knowledge he'd learned about palmistry could be utilized to help young people find occupations they'd be best suited for. William Benham spent the next thirty years developing the system he described in his book, *How to Choose Vocations from the Hand*. This book, published in 1932, used his system of classifying people into different types using the mounts. These seven types were modified further by locating a secondary mount, followed by a series of tests using the texture of the skin, the color, flexibility, consistency of the hands, the three worlds (mental, business, and material), and an examination of the fingers and thumb.

Since then, many palmists have explored this subject further, but as the annual Gallup reports show, even today few people are using palmistry, or any other method, to determine the type of career they'd be happiest and most successful in.

Here are some desirable qualities for people working in a variety of careers. These are intended to be guides, rather than absolutes. You can, for instance, find entrepreneurs with short fingers, but you'll also find many with long fingers. You'll also find people doing manual work who lack an angle of practicality.

Every now and again, you'll find people doing work that they know is not right for them. There could be any number of reasons for this. Consequently, it's impossible to look at a hand and tell the person what he or she is doing for a living.

However, what you can say is that someone would be well-suited for a career in such-and-such a field. The person will be impressed if he or she is working in that area. If he or she is doing something completely different, the person is likely to agree that the field you said they would be good at had always appealed to him or her.

Accounting

A long middle finger with a square or spatulate tip and a firm Saturn mount are useful for an accounting career. The head line should be long and straight. A good destiny line is useful, too.

Architecture

An architect should have a spatulate tip on a long ring finger. The first phalange on this finger should be the longest. The middle finger should be long and straight. The head line should be long, indicating love of detail. An angle of practicality is useful, too.

Armed Forces

Large, broad hands with thick, average-length fingers with square or spatulate tips are useful for people in the armed forces. The mounts of Mercury and inner and outer Mars should be firm. The palm should be flat. The thumb should be strong and straight with a pronounced tip phalange. There should be a slight gap between the head and life lines at their start.

A strong index finger is essential to rise to a commanding position.

Business Success

A good mount of Mercury and a long, straight little finger on a broad hand are signs of business acumen. A clear, well-marked health line shows the person will have the necessary stamina and energy to pursue his or her goals. As the hepatica heads toward the mount of Mercury, it is often related to business ability as well as health. A good-sized thumb with a wide angle between it and the hand enables the business person to relate well with others. A strong, straight, and preferably long, index finger provides common sense and integrity. A strong, straight middle finger provides seriousness and a desire to be rewarded for the effort put in. A firm palm is necessary as it shows the person can stand up for him or herself. The loop of good intent is useful for people in business, as it provides seriousness, reliability, and a hard work ethic.

A strong destiny line is useful in some careers, but I have met many successful business people who don't have this line. A destiny line is useful for business people who work in a specific field. Many entrepreneurial people change occupations regularly and this sometimes means they don't have a solid destiny line running down their palms. (Incidentally, I've seen strong destiny lines on the palms of beggars. This simply means they've made a lifetime career from begging.)

Cooking

There are many types of cooks ranging from people who struggle to prepare dinner for their families all the way to chefs at Michelin-Star restaurants. Consequently, people with every type of hand can learn to cook. However, some people, ranging from home cooks to professionals, are highly talented at the art. These people will have some of these qualities visible on their hands: broad hand, strong thumb and fingers, angle of practicality, padded bottom phalanges on the fingers, and a curving head line.

Engineer

The palm should be large and square with long knotty fingers. The fingertips should be spatulate or square. The mounts of Jupiter and Mercury should be strong and firm. The head line should be long and well-marked. The thumb should be long and contain an angle of practicality.

Healing

A strong indication of healing ability is the medical stigmata, a series of three to ten vertical lines on the mount of Mercury. People with these have a caring nature and often gravitate into a healing career. However, many people with these lines use them in different ways. Good gardeners have them, for instance, as do many people who are sympathetic, kind, and caring.

The mounts of Mercury, Jupiter, and Luna should be strong. A long head line that touches the life line at its start and a strong thumb are also helpful. The fingers should be long with knots between the second and third phalanges. A spatulate hand or fingertips are useful, too.

Many healers also have a sympathy line, which is a straight line that diagonally crosses the mount of Jupiter. It's in the same area as the Ring of Solomon but is straight, rather than curved.

Nurse's lines are fine vertical lines between the heart line and the fingers. They provide empathy and compassion for all living things and are frequently found on the hands of natural healers.

A wide space between the heart line and the fingers reveals a person who is more than happy to help people who are suffering. This person will be open, sympathetic, and kind-hearted.

People with a St. Andrew's cross in their palms often take up healing as a career.

Law

A good lawyer should have a well-developed little finger with a strong first phalange. The fingers and thumb should be long, and the index finger should be strong and straight. The writer's fork should be present on a long head line. A well-marked destiny line indicates the pursuit of a career, rather than simply an occupation. A wide quadrangle provides the ability to see both sides of a situation.

A judge should have long fingers with conic tips and a long tip phalange on the little finger. A straight index finger and a firm mount of Apollo shows the ability to administer justice tempered with mercy.

Managerial Ability

A good manager should have broad hands, a long straight index finger, and a long thumb. The mount of Jupiter should be firm. In addition, the manager should have a good tip on the Mercury finger to aid communication, a firm mount of Mercury, a firm second world, and a head line that heads toward the mount of Luna to encourage creativity.

Manual Dexterity

A broad palm with few lines and well-developed mounts of Mars and Venus indicate someone who is good at manual work. Other indications are a straight head line of any length, a wide life line that comes well across the palm, an angle of practicality, a broad square palm, and square or spatulate fingertips.

Sales Ability

Salespeople need good communication skills. Consequently, they need a well-developed mount of Mercury and a strong little finger with a long tip phalange. Conic fingertips help them communicate well with their customers. Square fingertips provide good business sense. If their hands also show signs of ambition, such as a strong index finger, salespeople with square fingertips will be looking for opportunities to progress in the organization. Salespeople also need a good ring finger to ingratiate themselves with potential customers. A good mount of Jupiter increases sociability and helps salespeople to get along well with their customers. A gap between the middle and ring fingers show that they can work well on their own. A strong thumb shows the ability to persist until the sale has been made. Many salespeople have long middle phalanges on their fingers. The upper and lower mounts of Mars should be well developed to provide resourcefulness and the ability to persist until the sale has been made. The third world mounts of Venus, Luna, and Neptune should also be strong to provide an instinctive sense of knowing when to push for a sale and when to hold back and provide more information.

Scientific Potential

Knotted fingers with conic or pointed tips on a square palm are often a sign of someone with an interest in science. The tip phalanges are usually the longest phalanges on each finger. Other indications are a long, straight, well-marked head line, a long little finger, and strong mounts of Saturn, Apollo, and Mercury.

Teaching Ability

A good teacher has a long little finger and well-developed mounts of Mercury and Jupiter. The tip phalange of the little finger should be long to give the teacher fluency with words. If all three phalanges of the middle finger are equal in length, the person will be a natural teacher.

The teacher's square that is sometimes found on the mount of Jupiter denotes someone who is born to teach. Ideally, the fingers are long and have conic tips. The head line should be long and have a writer's fork on the end. This enables him or her to come up with good ideas and explain them to others.

Teachers often have a medical stigmata under their little fingers as well, indicating the caring, humanitarian side of their natures. The loop of good intent is also frequently found in the hands of teachers.

How to Help People Find the Right Career

Given the huge numbers of people who are doing work they don't enjoy, one of the most useful things a palmist can do is to advise people on areas that would interest them and make use of their special abilities.

One way of doing this involves the shape of the hand (earth, air, fire, water, and d'Arpentigny's seven types), the most prominent mount, and the three worlds. The shape of the hands reveal the person's personality, the leading mount shows what he or she likes to do, and the three worlds show how the person can make use of this information to his or her best advantage.

Here's an example. Let's assume the person is a thirty-five-year-old man. He has an air hand, the mount of Mercury is prominent, as is the second world.

The air hand tells us that he is mentally alert, creative, conscientious, practical, and thoughtful.

The prominent mount of Mercury reveals that he's friendly and easy to get along with. He's shrewd and makes up his mind quickly. He's good at dealing with the public and would do well in business. He's interested in what's going on in the world around him, especially in matters relating to science and current affairs. He enjoys conversations about all the things he's interested in. He has good communication skills and will make good use of this in every area of his life. He's spontaneous and has a good sense of humor.

The second world shows that he can make good use of his personality and skills in the business world, either in management or in running his own business. He has the potential to do well financially and is also likely to gain satisfaction from helping people who are not as fortunate as he is. This strong humanitarian side of his nature shows that law and medicine are also fields he might be interested in pursuing.

Here's another example, this time of a young woman with a water hand, a strong mount of Apollo, and a prominent first world.

The water hand tells us that she is sensitive, emotional, sympathetic, and creative. She's also sensitive and easily hurt.

The prominent mount of Apollo reveals that she is enthusiastic, versatile, interested in beauty, and has good taste. She probably has many friends and enjoys socializing with them.

The first world shows that she could use her creativity and people skills. As she enjoys thinking and learning, she could use her significant creative skills (shown by both the shape of her hand and the mount of Apollo) to create beauty in some way or to encourage and teach others.

In these two examples, we've examined nothing but the shape of the hand, the prominent mount, and the three worlds. Naturally, the hands can reveal much more than that. In the second example, we found that the woman had significant creative potential. We could examine the hand further to discover if this talent was music, art, writing, or anything else. We could look at her thumb to see if she could stand up for herself and to determine if willpower or logic was stronger. Her index finger would tell us if she had the necessary drive and ambition to achieve success. We could check the consistency of her hands to see how much energy she has. We could determine how flexible her mind is by checking the flexibility of her hands. We could check her fingertips to finetune the various types of energy she has and how they're used. Her fingerprints would provide insight into her personality and purpose in life.

Money

Almost everyone is interested in money. Not surprisingly, it's one of the four major areas of interest for most people who visit palmists: money, love, health, and happiness. People can obtain money in a variety of ways. Most have to earn it, of course, and this can be done by working for someone else or through self-employment. Many people inherit money and some marry a person who already has money. A few people win large sums of money in a lottery. Some people make money by saving it and then investing it.

As a general rule, people who do well in their careers usually retire comfortably. However, this is not always the case. I know a successful lawyer who is still working in his middle-seventies as he can't afford to retire. He had an expensive divorce in his fifties, and before he'd fully recovered from that, he remarried and had three more children. Fortunately, he loves his work so much that he tells me he'll never be able to retire.

My former mailman retired in his late forties. He earned a fraction of my lawyer friend's income but saved a portion of what he earned and was able to retire early with three rental properties as well as his home.

Hand shapes play an important role in how people handle and deal with their money. People with earth hands are cautious with money and are good at saving it. They dislike spending it and usually manage to leave a goodly amount to their families when they die.

People with air hands are generally good with money and are willing to take calculated risks. Consequently, they can experience ups and downs financially at times but remain positive and confident that they'll ultimately do well.

People with fire hands are shrewd and invest wisely, often based on their hunches and feelings. They spread their investments around, being careful not to put all their money into one sector of the market.

People with water hands like the comforts of life and, as these are usually expensive, they need to make money. They usually do this by working in an aesthetic field, and many do well financially as a result.

People who have knots on the lower joints of the fingers have a down-to-earth approach to money. They enjoy earning it and are grateful for what money can do for them. After using however much is required for everyday life, they'll have fun with some of the remainder and will invest the rest.

A long little finger increases the person's financial potential. If this finger also happens to be bent or twisted, the person will be shrewd when it comes to money but may also be tempted to dishonesty.

Someone's financial potential can be seen in the money triangle in the center of the palm. Two sides of this triangle are formed by the head and destiny lines, and the third line is a short line on the percussion (little finger) side of the destiny line. The money triangle is usually small. It's a positive sign if the triangle is fully formed as this means the person can hold on to some of the money as it passes through him or her. If the triangle has a gap in it or there is no third side to the triangle, most of the money will escape.

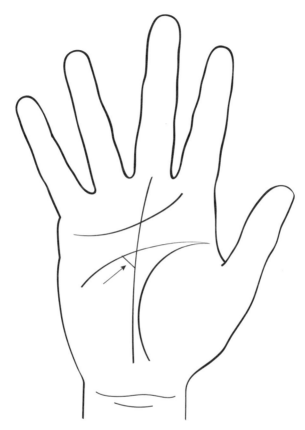

Figure 37: Money Triangle

A fine line running from the life line to one of the finger mounts shows how easily the money is earned. If the line runs to the mount of Jupiter, the person will enjoy great success in his or her career and may well be honored and recognized by his peers. If the line runs to the mount of Saturn, the person will earn his or her money through considerable effort and hard work. If it ends on the mount of Apollo, the person will be lucky with money but may be inclined to take unnecessary risks. Consequently, he or she will need to evaluate opportunities carefully. If the line ends on the mount of Mercury, the person will make money in business.

A wide space between the fingers where they join the palm is a sign that money will come and go quickly.

A clear unbroken vertical line about an inch in length running up and onto the mount of Mercury is a sign of good luck in financial matters. People with this sign can take calculated risks, as most of the time matters will work in their favor.

Useful Traits to Possess

Adaptability

Someone who can easily adjust to changing situations or circumstances is said to be adaptable. It's an extremely useful quality in today's world where most people have to change occupations or even careers a number of times as a result of the fast pace of life.

Loops in the fingerprints reveal someone who is sociable, agreeable, and adaptable. A flexible hand and a supple thumb are also signs of adaptability. A good mount of Apollo indicates an agreeable person who is able to adapt quickly when required.

Ambition

Someone with a strong desire for success is said to be ambitious. He or she is prepared to set goals and do whatever is necessary to achieve them. Not everyone is ambitious, but it's fortunate that many people are, as ambitious people are the ones who create opportunities for everyone else.

The index finger and the mount of Jupiter are the first two indications of drive and ambition. The index finger should be straight and at least as long as the ring finger. The second phalange of this finger should be the longest. The thumb should be long and strong. The mount of Jupiter should be firm and prominent. Some people have a fine line of ambition that crosses this mount and heads toward the base of the finger. This line is usually about half an inch long, but occasionally you'll find one that starts on the life line and runs all the way to the Jupiter finger.

A clear, well-marked destiny line can also be a sign of ambition, though it would have to be accompanied by a strong thumb and a good index finger.

Ambitious people often have a gap between their head and life lines. This denotes independence, but also reveals someone who is self-reliant and willing to take calculated risks.

Analytical Approach

Someone who is analytical enjoys analyzing and examining all the parts that make up the whole. They're not content with the overall picture and aren't happy until they've evaluated all the fine details.

People with knotted fingers are analytical. A straight or slightly curving head line also indicates an analytical thinker. Fingernails that are wider than they are long also show that the person is highly analytical, as well as outspoken and critical. People with long fingers enjoy details and tend to be analytical in their approach

Animals

People who relate well with animals often have a loop of inspiration on the mount of Neptune, an ulnar loop ("loop of nature") on the mount of Luna, or the loop of humor between the little and ring fingers. A medical stigmata, nurse's lines, and a wide quadrangle are beneficial, too.

Benevolence

Someone with a benevolent nature is a kind, caring, humanitarian person enjoys helping others.

Benevolence is indicated by smooth fingers, a well-developed mount of Venus with few worry lines on it, and a long curving head line.

Calmness

A calm person always seems to be in a peaceful state and remains tranquil even when other people are feeling agitated, angry, or excited.

People with smooth hands are able to remain calm and unruffled in most situations. A strong mount of outer Mars also provides calmness as the person has good self-control and the ability to stand up for him or herself. Square fingertips provide the person with a calm, common-sense approach to life.

Common Sense

Someone with common sense shows good practical judgment that does not depend on education or specialized knowledge. Tryon Edwards (1819–1894), the American theologian, said, "Common sense is, of all kinds, the most uncommon. It implies good judgment, sound discretion, and true and practical wisdom applied to common life."

People with broad, square palms are stable, reliable, down-to-earth, and show good common sense. The loop of common sense is another good indication of this trait. A straight middle finger also endows its owner with common sense. A square tip on the thumb is another indicator of common sense. A writer's fork on the head line often creates common sense as the person can see both sides of a situation and, after considering them, make a good decision.

Communication Skills

People with good communication skills have long index and little fingers, a long curving head line, and well-developed, firm mounts of Luna and Mercury. A spatulate fingertip on the Apollo finger is useful, too.

Confidence

Someone with confidence is self-reliant and believes in his or her own abilities.

A strong index finger provides confidence, as does a strong thumb. A wide angle of the thumb provides confidence, as it helps the person to believe in him or herself. A well-rounded, firm, but not overly high Jupiter mount also provides confidence. When the hand is held naturally, a wide space between the index and middle fingers denotes confidence.

Conservatism

Conservative people want to preserve the existing status quo and make gradual improvements. They won't act until they've carefully considered every aspect of the situation.

Conservatism is indicated when the heart and head lines are close together and the head line is attached to the life line at its start. Usually, the fingers are set close together.

Courage

Courageous people can withstand danger, pain, and other difficulties. They experience fear but are able to overcome it. They are brave, resolute, and strong. People with moral courage act in accordance with their beliefs despite criticism and opposition from others.

The mount of inner Mars reveals how courageous a person is. It should be firm and strong. Occasionally, a loop of courage can be found on this mount. This shows that the person is totally fearless and will fight to the very end for something he or she believes in. Both mounts of Mars should be firm.

Diplomacy

Diplomatic people utilize skill and tact in their dealings with others, especially in delicate situations.

A "waisted" second phalange on the thumb is a sign of tact and diplomacy. People with water hands are generally diplomatic, as are people with clear heart lines that end between the index and middle fingers. Silky skin is a sign of a gentle, cultured person who will tend to be diplomatic. Droplets like tiny drops of water on the fingertips when the hand is held palm downward are a sign of sensitivity and diplomacy.

Energy

Energy is revealed by the thumb. People with a large first phalange possess a great deal of willpower and energy. The size and height of the mount of Venus also reveals how much energy the person has at his or her disposal. People with life lines that swoop well across their palms have much more energy than people who have life lines that hug their thumbs. However, the area enclosed by the life line also needs to be firm for this energy to be fully utilized. A well-developed mount of Jupiter also provides the person with energy.

Friendliness

A friendly person is kindly, caring, supportive, and helpful to others. Everyone has the capacity to be friendly, but some people are more open and friendly than others. People with conic palms or fingertips, a curving heart line, a wide life line, and a strong, firm mount of Venus are good examples of this. A firm mount of Mercury and a well-set little finger encourage communication.

Generosity

Generous people are magnanimous, unselfish, and give freely to others. Generosity means much more than money. People can be generous with their time, possessions, and affections, as well as money.

Generosity is revealed by the angle the thumb makes to the side of the hand. The greater the angle, the more generous the person will be. The angle is called the "angle of generosity." Most people have an angle of forty to forty-five degrees, which shows that they're reasonably generous but are also careful. People with a ninety-degree angle are overly generous and can be taken advantage of by others. People with flexible thumbs and supple fingers that bend backward under pressure are also kind and generous.

Gratitude

Gratitude is a feeling of being thankful and appreciative for any acts of kindness.

Gratitude is indicated by the Apollo lines, the short vertical lines immediately below the ring (Apollo) finger. These show that the person feels grateful and expresses gratitude for all the good things in his or her life.

Many years ago, a friend of mine started a gratitude journal when she was recovering from depression. Each day she wrote down at least ten things she was grateful for. This process helped her recovery, but it also had an unexpected side effect—she gained Apollo lines in her hand. She is now happily married with a family, but still writes in her gratitude journal every evening before going to bed.

Happiness

When people are happy, they experience joy, pleasure, contentment, and gladness. Obviously, no one is happy all the time. However, some fortunate people have a happy disposition and bounce back quickly when they experience the inevitable sad and down times. People with conic hands or fingertips usually look on the bright side of life. A strong, firm mount of Apollo and a curving heart line with few islands on it also encourage happiness.

Honesty

People who are honest are trustworthy, truthful, honorable, and sincere.

Honesty is shown in the little finger. If this finger is short and crooked, the person will have a tendency to be dishonest. A strong, straight little finger denotes honesty. However, that being said, everyone tells lies at times. Someone with a straight little finger will be honest but might not hesitate to tell a lie to prevent hurting someone's feelings.

Humor

People with a sense of humor appreciate and express anything that they find amusing or comical.

The loop of humor is situated between the little and ring fingers and indicates someone who is cheerful, positive, optimistic, good-natured, and fun-loving. People with this loop enjoy spending time with people to share a laugh. A well-developed mount of Mercury gives people a good sense of humor. One or more whorls in the fingerprints also provides a humorous approach to everyday life. A wide angle of the thumb is a common factor in many professional comedians, and this enables them to express themselves in a humorous way.

Idealism

Idealistic people treasure and pursue their vision of perfection. They have high principles and strive to live up to them.

People with philosopher's hands are idealistic and strive to improve the world in some way. If the heart line curves and ends under the index finger, the person will be idealistic and dream of a perfect relationship. Unfortunately, no one can live up to these expectations, which means life will seldom be easy for this person.

Pointed fingertips, especially when found on long, thin fingers, are a strong indication of an idealistic personality.

Imagination

Everyone possesses an imagination and can create mental visions or images in their minds.

A well-developed mount of Luna and a head line that curves toward it show that the person possesses a good imagination and is creative, original, and inventive.

Independence

Independence is shown by the amount of space between the fingers when the hand is held out open and relaxed. A wide gap between the index and middle fingers reveals an independent thinker; between the middle and ring fingers, independence in all situations; and between the ring and little fingers, independent action. A destiny line that starts well away from the life line and a gap between the head and life lines at their start also indicate independence.

Influence

Someone with influence is able to affect other people by intangible or indirect means. He or she is usually in a position of authority and has power and influence. This rare quality is revealed by a strong, straight index finger and full and firm mounts. The Jupiter mount should be the most prominent of these. In addition, the thumb should be strong and straight with a long tip phalange.

Integrity

Integrity comes from the Latin word *integritas*, which means "whole." Someone with integrity is honest, loyal, decent, kind, and incorruptible. This person will have strong moral principles and do everything he or she can to live a good, honest, upright life.

People with integrity have a strong mount of inner Mars. A mount of Saturn that is displaced toward the index finger also indicates integrity. A centrally placed apex on the mount of Jupiter is a strong indication of integrity.

Intuition

Intuition is the act of receiving information without using any conscious reasoning. It is revealed on the hand in a number of ways. A strong line of intuition is one. People with water hands are likely to be more sensitive and aware than people with other types of hands. A head line that curves up to and sometimes into the mount of Luna is a sign that the person acts on his or her hunches and feelings. A mystic cross in the quadrangle shows the potential for the person to make good use of his or her psychic ability. A loop of inspiration provides the person with plenty of intuition.

An eye-shaped island on the crease between the first and second phalanges of the thumb is a sign of mystical or psychic ability. It is sometimes called "Buddha's Eye."

Inventive Ability

Long first phalanges on knotted fingers are an indication of inventive ability. This is enhanced if the palms or fingers are spatulate.

Kindness

Kind people are considerate, generous, gentle, helpful, thoughtful, understanding, and friendly. The German poet, Johann Wolfgang von Goethe (1748–1832), wrote, "Kindness is the golden chain by which society is held together."

Kindness is revealed by a firm mount of Venus, a sympathy line, or ring of Solomon on a fine and silky-textured hand.

Loyalty

People who are loyal are faithful to their friends, country, government, or cause. They are dependable, devoted, reliable, staunch, and unwavering.

Loyalty is revealed by a square palm with long fingers, square or spatulate fingertips, and square fingernails. The thumb should also be long with a square tip and thumbnail. The fingers should be set close together on the palm. The heart line curves and ends under the index finger.

Motivation

Motivated people possess the necessary desire, ambition, and drive to achieve their goals.

A fine, clearly marked destiny line is found in the palms of most motivated people. However, some motivated people do not have this line. They are non-conformists who follow their own path through life, marching to the beat of a different drummer. They are motivated by anything that interests and fascinates them. Motivated people also have strong thumbs, straight index and ring fingers, and firm mounts of Mars.

Patience

Patient people have the ability to endure difficult situations without annoyance, aggravation, complaint, or loss of temper. They manage to keep calm and composed in almost every type of situation.

Patience is revealed by long fingers, a large mount of Luna, and a firm mount of outer Mars. A smooth mount of Saturn also indicates patience.

Persistence

People with persistence continue working steadily toward their goals no matter what setbacks or opposition they receive.

Persistence is often revealed by a large, strong thumb. A broad, square palm also denotes someone with plenty of determination and persistence.

Positive Outlook

Cheerful, positive people have prominent Apollo and Mercury mounts, a wide space between their ring and middle fingers, and a long, straight ring finger. A long first phalange on the little finger and a good mount of Jupiter are useful too, as they enhance the ability to get on well with others.

Practicality

Practicality is revealed by square fingers on a broad palm, a long thumb, an angle of practicality, and a straight head line. Earth, elementary, and square hands are all indications of practicality.

Psychic Ability

As everyone experiences hunches and feelings, we all possess psychic ability and have the potential to develop it further if we wish. However, some people are naturally more gifted in this area than others and are likely to possess some of these signs in their palms: a strong mount of Luna, line of intuition, pointed fingertips, firm finger mounts, a mystic cross in the quadrangle, a ring of Solomon on the mount of Jupiter, a triangle on the mount of Luna, and a dermatoglyphic pattern, such as a loop or whorl, on the mount of Luna. A head line that swoops up toward a strong mount of Luna enhances both intuition and creativity.

Another strong indication of psychic ability is a fine semi-circular line that starts on the mount of outer Mars and finishes on the mount of Luna. It's sometimes called the "intuition crescent."

Resourcefulness

Someone who is resourceful is reliable, capable, and full of initiative. He or she is able to deal with problems and concerns quickly and skillfully.

Resourcefulness is indicated by supple fingers, strong finger mounts, a good length little finger, preferably with a conic tip, and a thumb angle of at least forty-five degrees.

Responsibility

Someone who is responsible is conscientious, dependable, reliable, sensible, and stable. He or she is accountable for his or her actions and decisions.

Responsible people have all, or most of, these aspects: firm palms, long, straight middle fingers, strong thumbs, firm mounts of Mars, long destiny lines, strong unyielding thumbs, and loops of common sense.

Self-Esteem

People with good self-esteem respect themselves and maintain a favorable opinion of themselves in every type of situation.

Self-esteem is indicated by a straight index finger, a firm mount of Venus, and well-marked heart, head, and life lines.

Sympathy

Sympathetic people feel and understand what other people are going through. They are caring, concerned, compassionate, and understanding.

The sympathy line is a short straight line immediately below the index finger that reveals someone who is kind-hearted, sympathetic, and enjoys helping others.

Tact

Tactful people have the ability to deal with people in an understanding and considerate manner. They instinctively know what to say or do in difficult or upsetting situations. They are able to say what needs to be said without offending or upsetting others.

Tact is indicated by a waisted second phalange on the thumb and a heart line that curves and ends between the index and middle fingers.

Tolerance

People who are tolerant accept that because everyone is different, other people have the right to their own views and opinions. They are unprejudiced and free from bigotry.

Tolerance is indicated by a wide angle between the thumb and the side of the hand. A wide quadrangle (the area between the heart and head lines) also reveals someone who is tolerant.

Trust

Trusting people believe in the goodness, honesty, and integrity of others. The Scottish author George MacDonald (1824–1905) wrote, "To be trusted is a greater compliment than to be loved" (*The Marquis of Lossie*).

People who are trusting are likely to have flexible fingers and thumb, a wide quadrangle, a curving heart line, a wide angle of the thumb, and a firm mount of Jupiter.

Versatility

Someone who is versatile has many different skills and can move quickly from one task to another.

Versatility is indicated by long little and ring fingers, flexible fingers, and spatulate fingertips. The presence of a Sun line creates versatility, and this is increased if there are two or more of these fine lines on the palm.

Willpower

Someone with willpower is controlled, self-disciplined, and determined to achieve his or her goals using single-mindedness and strength of will.

The tip section of the thumb indicates willpower. Consequently, the thumb should be firm and large with a long tip. The palm and fingers should be firm.

Don't Hide Your Talents

The world has a population of almost eight billion people. Every one of these people possesses talents that can be developed and used to improve their lives and, in most cases, the lives of others. Unfortunately, many people either don't recognize their talents or choose not to use them. There can be many reasons for this.

Individual circumstances vary. Someone who is struggling to support a family on minimum pay is not likely to have much time to develop a musical talent, for instance. Someone suffering from chronic ill health is also likely to have little time or energy to develop a talent.

Sadly, though, most people who fail to develop their talents do so because of fear, doubt, and worry. Many years ago, I helped life insurance salespeople overcome their reluctance to make cold phone calls. They were intelligent people who had undergone full training before starting their new careers. They knew that if they kept making phone calls, sooner or later someone would agree to see them, and that if they made a certain number of appointments, they'd get a sale.

This was fine in theory, but these salespeople found it impossible to make another phone call after a series of rejections. Of course, some people hung up on them, a few were rude, but most simply said they weren't interested. They usually managed to make about a dozen phone calls before they gave up. Their problem was "fear, doubt, and worry."

They were scared to make another phone call as they didn't like being rejected. Of course, they knew they weren't being rejected—the person was rejecting the product, not them. They started having doubts about their ability to succeed at selling life insurance. They worried that they wouldn't make any money in commission sales. Each rejection made it harder for them to pick up the phone again. Fortunately, I was able to help many of these people who went on to make a successful career in life insurance.

Over the years, I've met many people who have been crippled by "fear, doubt, and worry." No wonder they find it hard to utilize their potential.

These negative traits are visible on the palm but will disappear if the person is motivated enough to work on them. Here are some of the negative traits that might be holding you back.

Anxiety, Worry, and Stress

People who suffer from anxiety are worried and tense. They live in a state of uneasiness and fear, worrying about the past, present, and future. Meditation, relaxation, and self-hypnosis are all good ways to help people suffering from anxiety.

Worry lines are fine lines radiating from the base of the thumb toward the life line. Some people have none of these, while others appear to have dozens. Someone who worries about everything will have plenty of worry lines on his or her hands. Someone who worries only when there's cause for worry may have just a few lines, and people who don't worry at all will have virtually none.

Palms covered with a network of fine lines are the classic indication of anxiety and worry. Stress is indicated by fine horizontal lines on the tip phalanges of the fingers. They gradually appear when the person is suffering from undue stress and slowly disappear once the difficulties have been resolved. If these lines appear on the second or third phalanges, it's a sign that the anxiety and stress could cause health problems if the matter is not resolved. Often these lines appear on one finger, which provides information about the particular area of life that is causing the problem.

Stress is also indicated by a poor-quality section of the head line. It will look furry or fuzzy for the period that the person is stressed. The same effect can be seen on the life line when the person's health has been affected by prolonged stress. The heart line can also show this if the person is suffering from emotional stress.

Vertical ridges on the fingernails are a sign of anxiety.

Islands on the head line can be a sign of headaches caused by stress.

Chapter Eleven
Leadership in the Hand

A leader is someone who has the necessary ability or authority to guide, direct, or inspire others.

Leadership qualities are indicated by a strong Jupiter mount and a long second phalange on the preferably long index (Jupiter) finger. A star of Jupiter on the mount increases the person's drive and ambition to reach the top in his or her field. A long, strong, low-set thumb which forms a wide angle to the palm is also a sign of a natural leader. A clear, preferably long, destiny line that heads toward the middle finger and a life line that sweeps well out into the palm are also useful for anyone in a leadership role, as they provide stamina and a sense of direction. A strong little finger provides the ability to motivate, persuade, and influence others. People with fire hands frequently make natural leaders.

Several years ago, a good friend of mine asked me to help him decide if any of his managerial team were capable of taking on a leadership role in his business. It was an interesting request, as although he employed more than one hundred people, Don was a hands-on, controlling CEO who trusted no one and found it hard to delegate. Consequently, although he had a management team, none of them were really managers, as Don micromanaged everything and was the only person able to make decisions about anything relating to the business. Few managers could put up with this for long, and most left after a year of two. None of his current managers had been with the company for more than two years.

Don was an entrepreneur. He'd started his logistics business twenty-five years earlier with a small truck and a dream. He had an earth hand and frequently told me that the best days of his life had been when he was struggling to get established in a highly competitive market. His short fingers, stubborn thumb, and short, straight head line were useful when he started his business, but meant his personality was too impulsive and abrasive when it came to running a large business that worked internationally. Don is an extremely outgoing and entertaining person to meet socially, but I could imagine how difficult it would be to work for him.

He was planning to hold a dinner for all his employees and their partners to celebrate the company's twenty-fifth birthday. There'd be a band and other entertainment. He asked me if I'd read palms as part of the entertainment, and while doing this, see what leadership qualities I could find in three of his managers. This was because he didn't want the staff to know that he was using palmistry to evaluate them.

I explained that anything I learned as a result of looking at someone's palms was confidential, and that I couldn't pass on information about anyone without their permission. I thought this was the end of the matter, but in his excitable, impulsive way, Don was unable to keep it a secret. During a managers' meeting, he told them of his friendship with me, and how he'd been helped by my knowledge of his palms. He explained that he had a new role in mind and wanted to appoint someone who was already working for the business rather than recruit someone from outside. He asked if any of the managers would agree to have me look at their hands and let him know what I'd found.

Three of the eight managers were excited by the idea, but the others raised objections. One objected on religious grounds, one was concerned about the accuracy of palmistry, and the others simply felt uneasy about the whole idea. However, by the end of the meeting, they'd agreed to have me read palms at the company dinner. After seeing me read palms, and presumably after they'd spoken to staff members who'd had a reading, they'd have another meeting and decide whether or not they'd let me look at their palms.

The dinner was a huge success. In the early part of the evening, several magicians and I worked the tables. They did card tricks and I read palms. After dinner, there was a standup comedian, followed by dancing. During the evening, Don introduced me to a few people and asked me to read their palms, but I had no idea if they were part of his management team.

A few weeks later, I was invited to attend a meeting where Don told the eight managers his plans for the future of the business. He was intending to become the chairman and was looking for someone to take over the role of CEO. Disbelief was followed by several gentle jokes about how Don would be unable to let go of the day to day operation of the business. Don explained that one of his sons was seriously ill, and the real reason for stepping sideways was because he wanted to spend more time with his family.

He then asked me to tell them what I'd be looking for if I read their palms. Fortunately, they'd all heard good things about my readings at the dinner, and when I explained that I wasn't fortune telling, but would be looking for leadership potential, everyone agreed to let me see their palms. I returned the next day and took palm prints.

While all of this was going on, I read everything I could find on leadership. Unfortunately, much of it wasn't particularly helpful. After all, how can you compare the personalities and leadership styles of people as diverse as John F. Kennedy, Nelson Mandela, Winston Churchill, Angela Merkel, Margaret Thatcher, Mahatma Gandhi, Napoleon Bonaparte, and Florence Nightingale?

Leaders come in all sorts of varieties. Some are natural leaders from birth, while others discover their potential much later in life when they're forced to take on a leadership role. Some are extroverts, while others are introverted. Height, weight, gender, color, and personality have no bearing on someone's leadership potential.

There are a virtually unlimited number of qualities that would be useful for a leader to possess.

I started by looking for quotations on leadership. One I particularly like is by Robert Townsend: "True leadership must be for the benefit of the followers, not the enrichment of the leaders." Ronald Reagan, the fortieth president of the United States, said, "Surround yourself with the best people you can find, delegate authority, and don't interfere as long as the policy you've decided upon is being carried out." Ralph Lauren, the American clothing designer, said: "A leader has the vision and conviction that a dream can be achieved. He inspires the power and energy to get it done."

Eventually, I came up with a list of ten qualities that I thought every leader should have: integrity, ability to inspire others, passion, courage, communication skills, accountability, creativity, ability to delegate, relentless positivity, and ability to focus on the future.

Integrity

Integrity is an essential quality. Oprah Winfrey said it all: "Real integrity is doing the right thing, knowing that nobody's going to know whether you did it or not." A true leader always does the right thing and acts fairly, honestly, and honorably. If you're not honest yourself, you can't expect the people who work for you to be honest either.

Inspiration

A leader has to know how to motivate and inspire others. You can inspire others by putting joy and passion into everything you do. You need to remain positive and calm no matter what problems you encounter. Motivation and inspiration are contagious. As Lee Iacocca said, "Motivation is everything. You can do the work of two people, but you can't be two people. Instead, you have to inspire the next guy down the line and get him to inspire his people."

Passion

Donovan Bailey, the Jamaican athlete, said, "Follow your passion, be prepared to work hard and sacrifice, and, above all, don't let anyone limit your dreams." A leader needs to be passionate about what he or she does. You can't inspire or motivate anyone if you're not fully committed to your goal.

Courage

A leader needs courage to achieve his or her goals. Walt Disney said, "Courage is the main quality of leadership, in my opinion, no matter where it is exercised."

Communication Skills

A leader can't achieve anything until he or she has communicated his or her vision to the rest of the workforce. Words can motivate and sway others. The American lawyer James Humes said, "The art of communication is the language of leadership."

Accountability

It's natural to make excuses or try to assign blame, but leaders accept responsibility and are accountable for whatever has occurred. Leaders take ownership of their mistakes as well as the mistakes of their team. Winston Churchill said, "The price of greatness is responsibility." Leaders also ensure that every member of the team is accountable for his or her work and provide regular feedback on how they are progressing.

Creativity

Leaders need to motivate and encourage their team to be creative and to come up with innovative ideas.

Delegation

Leaders must be able to delegate tasks to others, as it's impossible for them to do everything themselves. The art of delegation is to choose the right people and to let them get on with the job without checking up on them every five minutes. The American author John C. Maxwell puts it: "If you want to do a few small things right, do them yourself. If you want to do great things, and make a big impact, learn to delegate."

Positivity

It's impossible to motivate and inspire others without being positive yourself. Willie Nelson said, "Once you replace negative thoughts with positive ones, you'll start having positive results." Leaders need to maintain a positive attitude to motivate themselves and everyone they work with.

Focus on the Future

Leaders need to be forward-looking people. They have to handle their day-to-day responsibilities while remaining clearly focused on the future they desire. They're visionaries who study future trends, visualize their ideal future, and make plans to ensure their vision becomes a reality.

Finding Leadership Traits in the Hand

Fortunately, all of these qualities can be found on the hands.

Integrity is revealed by a long and straight little finger and well-developed mounts of Mercury and Apollo. A mount of Saturn that is displaced toward the index finger, a centrally placed apex on the mount of Jupiter, and a strong mount of inner Mars are all signs of integrity.

People with strong conic-tipped index fingers, a mystic cross on the mount of Jupiter, and a strong mount of Mercury have the ability to inspire and motivate others.

Passion is indicated by a strong, firm mount of Venus encircled by a well-marked life line and a firm mount of Apollo. People with spatulate fingertips also have an abundance of enthusiasm, passion, and energy.

Courage is indicated by the firmness of the two mounts of Mars, particularly the mount of inner Mars. This should be firm and strong. It's even better if the loop of courage is also on this mount. This shows that the person is totally fearless and will never stop pursuing anything he or she believes in.

Communication skills are indicated by a long, straight little finger. This finger should reach up to at least the base phalange of the ring finger. If the little finger is set low on the palm, it should be mentally raised to the base of the ring finger. The Mercury mount should be firm and prominent. A clear hepatica line is also a sign of a good communicator. People with air hands are natural communicators who frequently choose careers that involve their communication skills.

Accountability is indicated by a strong, straight Saturn finger, a wide quadrangle, and a long destiny line.

Creativity is indicated in a variety of ways that we discussed in the previous chapter. These include a well-developed mount of Luna and a curving head line.

Positivity is indicated by prominent Apollo and Mercury mounts, a wide space between the ring and middle fingers, and a long, straight ring finger. A long first phalange on the little finger and a good mount of Jupiter are useful, too, as they enhance the person's ability to get on well with others.

The ability to delegate is indicated by small, smooth hands. People with small hands enjoy being involved in large-scale projects and must be able to delegate, as there is far too much information involved for one person to handle. A gap between the head and life lines at their start enhances the ability to delegate.

Examining the handprints for potential leadership ability was a fascinating experience. All eight people possessed most of the qualities I was looking for. This wasn't surprising, as they were all department managers.

One print was different, though. It was a small hand belonging to the only female manager Don had on his team. She had an air hand with long index and little fingers. The mounts of Jupiter, Apollo, and Mercury were all well developed. Her long and waisted thumb created a wide angle with the side of the palm. She had plenty of energy and stamina, as revealed by the large mount of Venus. Her destiny line started a third of the way down the palm and almost reached the mount of Saturn. The head line was long and curved toward the mount of Luna. There was a writer's fork at the end of this line. She had a whorl fingerprint pattern on the index finger of her right hand, and loops on the other fingers. The tri-radius was centrally situated at the top of the mount of Jupiter.

I recommended her for the new position. Don was concerned about this, as she wasn't one of the three people he was initially going to choose from. He had some sexist attitudes, as well, and expressed doubt that a woman would be able to lead a logistics company. Don was famous for making instant decisions, but in this case, he thought about it for three months before appointing her to the position. She's been a great success, and the company has more than doubled in size since she took on the role of CEO.

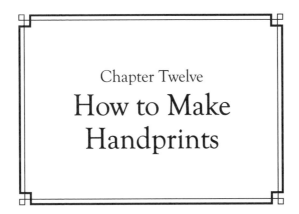

Chapter Twelve
How to Make Handprints

You'll find it helpful to create a library of handprints of the people you have read for. This enables you to build up a collection that you can refer to when necessary.

If someone returns to you for another reading, for instance, you'll be able to compare how his or her hands have changed since you last saw them. I took palm prints of my children's hands as they were growing up and it was fascinating to see how their different interests and potentials revealed themselves when they were still very young.

You'll be able to see if someone inherited his or her talents from a mother, father, or maybe a grandparent. You'll be able to see how certain traits have been passed on from generation to generation. You'll be able to detect similarities in the palms of people working in the same field.

You'll be able to see health factors more easily in a palm print than you can by examining the palm.

You can measure time more accurately on a print than you can from the hand itself.

You can also do original research. If you find an unusual marking on someone's hand, you can check your collection of prints to see if anyone you've read for before has the same marking. If you've discovered something new, you'll have a permanent record of it and may be able to contribute something valuable to the art.

Your growing collection will be a valuable resource that you'll refer to often. Every time you examine a palm print, you'll notice something that you'd overlooked before.

Taking a Print

You'll need a supply of good quality bond paper at least 8.5" × 11" (or the European A4 size). You'll also need a tube of artist's water-based black ink and an ink roller about four inches wide. You can buy these at any artist's supply store or online.

In addition to this, you'll need a slightly spongy surface to put the paper on. Many years ago, I started using a stack of tea towels folded in half, and I still use them today, as they work well. Prior to that I used a large piece of soft rubber that had supported an old-fashioned typewriter. Foam rubber is readily available and works well. The surface needs to be slightly spongy, as this enables you to take a print of the hollow of the hand.

Start by placing a sheet of paper on top of your stack of tea towels or other flexible surface.

Squeeze a small amount of ink onto a pane of glass or a spare sheet of bond paper. Roll it with the roller until the ink is smooth and the roller is covered with an even coating of ink.

Ask the people whose prints you are taking to remove their rings if possible, and to hold their hands palms-upward in front of you. Starting from the wrist, cover the palms with a fine coating of ink using long, even strokes of the roller. If the person has a deep hollow in the middle of his or her palms, you might have to use small, fine movements to ensure the entire surface of the palm is evenly covered.

Tell the person to hold his or her hands naturally and to place both hands simultaneously onto the sheet of paper that's resting on the tea towels. Press down gently on the backs of their hands to ensure that the middle of the palm makes an impression on the paper.

If you wish, you can use a pencil to make an outline of the palm to record its shape.

Hold down each end of the paper and ask the person to raise both hands straight upward. This reveals the print and you'll be able to see if it's good enough to use.

If the center of the palm has failed to leave an impression, you'll need to do it again. This time, after they've placed both hands on the paper, ask them to raise both hands in the air with the paper still attached. Gently press the paper into the hollow of their palms, and then carefully pull the paper off their hands.

Palm prints reveal only the side of the thumb. Consequently, you'll need to take separate prints of them.

You'll find that most people you read for will want to take their palm prints away with them. Consequently, I always ask if I can make an extra print for my files. Most people are happy for me to do this, but occasionally someone will refuse. There is no need to ink the hand again to make another print.

I identify and date the prints on the print itself. I also make notes about the firmness, coarseness, flexibility, height of the mounts, presence or absence of knots, information about the fingernails, and anything else I feel is relevant about the person's hands on a separate sheet of paper. I keep these with the prints for future reference.

It takes practice, but you'll soon be able to make perfect prints almost every time. It's easier to take prints of the hands separately, but I don't do this as I prefer to have both hands on the same sheet of paper.

Once you've taken the prints, escort the person to the bathroom and turn on the cold tap. Water-based ink comes off right away if the person simply holds his or her hands under cold running water. After this, your client can wash his or her hands with soap and warm water. You'll find that starting with cold water makes the job easier and faster than starting with soap and warm water. It also keeps the basin clean.

I file the prints alphabetically using the person's surname. Some palmists file their prints based on different features revealed in the hands. This is useful for research but makes it difficult to quickly find someone's prints when he or she returns for another reading.

Chapter Thirteen
How to Give a Palmistry Reading

Because of its associations with fortune telling, people have a wide variety of feelings and expectations when they come for a reading. Some are nervous and worried that the reader might pick up some guilty secret from their past. Others are concerned that he or she might tell them something terrible about their future or the future of their loved ones. I've even read for people who thought I'd know exactly when they were going to die.

Some expect the palmist to look at their hands and then speak nonstop for an hour, telling them all about their past, present, and future. Over the years, I've had a number of people refuse to speak until after I'd finished the reading. I assume they were doing this to test me, but they would have received a better reading if they'd asked a few questions or made a comment or two while I was doing the reading.

In actuality, a palmistry reading is a conversation between two people. It's an intimate experience, and one that should empower the person having the reading. People seldom come for a full-length reading when everything is going well in their lives. It's only when something bad has happened or they're seeking confirmation about a certain course of action that they'll book a private reading. During the reading, the client is able to discuss whatever is bothering him or her, and the reader can respond with advice based on what he or she sees in the client's hands.

You'll find no lack of volunteers if you simply mention your interest in the subject. People are always keen to have a free reading. Explain that you're still a novice and start by giving brief readings. This will enable you to see many palms in a short period of time. Even if your first readings are only sixty seconds long, the people you read for will still be thrilled with your knowledge and insight into their character.

Gradually, as you gain experience in the art, you'll be able to increase both the length and quality of your readings. When you reach this stage, you'll be able to help, counsel, and give advice to others.

At this point, you might decide to make a career out of palmistry, pursue it as a hobby, or maybe offer readings on a part-time basis. Whatever you do, you'll find your knowledge of palmistry extremely useful in your everyday life.

There are certain requirements that should be considered before deciding to become a reader. If you're going to read palms for others, you need to have a strong desire to help them. You must also be honest and discreet.

You can't say anything that could cause your clients worry and stress later on. An aunt of mine had a palm reading when she was a teenager. The palmist told her that she'd die at the age of sixty-five. This didn't worry her much then, as it was so far away. However, as she got into her sixties she started worrying about it, and when she turned sixty-five she was convinced she was going to die. Fortunately, the palm reader wasn't correct, but my aunt had several stressful and worrying years before she turned sixty-six as a result of her careless words.

For many years, I read palms at corporate events. These were quick, fun readings and I was booked as part of the entertainment. Occasionally, I'd read for someone whose palms I'd read years earlier and be amazed at how much they remembered from the previous reading. The same thing will happen when you start giving readings. Because of this, the most important rule of palm reading is to be gentle and kind. Don't say anything that could worry or frighten people.

I always stress the positive when giving a reading, as I want my clients to feel better about themselves afterward. I do this with both the fun and the serious readings. It's easy to do this when giving brief, five-minute, fun readings, as you can overlook anything negative you might see in the palm and focus on the person's positive traits. In the first place, it's not appropriate to mention anything negative in a party-type situation, and secondly, you might be wrong.

Frequently, in a social situation, the person you are reading for will have friends listening in on the reading. This is another reason why you must be upbeat, encouraging, and positive, even if you're convinced the person has grievous defects in his or her character or is about to experience difficulties in his or her life.

Naturally, when giving a full-length, private reading, you can discuss anything that the client wants to know, and you need to be honest. Even then, you have a duty to phrase your words carefully and be kind and caring.

As well as being caring and kind, you need to be empathetic and nonjudgmental. You can't make moral judgments. Sometimes clients will open up and tell you things they'd never tell anyone else.

It's important to be discreet and keep everything a client tells you confidential.

As most people are at least slightly nervous when having their palms read, when people come to see me privately, I try to put them at ease before looking at their palms. I start by telling them something about palmistry and what it can and can't do. I also tell them that their hands can and will change—because their future is up to them. I stress that they have the ability to create the future they desire as long as they're prepared to do whatever is necessary to achieve it.

After this, I look at their hands. I examine both sides of each hand, checking flexibility, texture, and firmness. I look at the fingernails and see if the fingers are held closed together or apart. I also look at the length of the fingers and how they're set on the palm. I look for a creative curve and the angles of practicality and pitch. While doing this I classify the hands (usually into earth, air, fire, or water, but sometimes into one of d'Arpentigny's classifications). I chat to the client while doing this, telling him or her what I'm doing and why I'm doing it.

I then ink the client's hands and make palm prints. I start looking at the dermatoglyphics on the print while the client is washing his or her hands. Many years ago, I could read the skin ridge patterns without even wearing glasses, but nowadays I use a magnifying glass to see them properly.

Once the client returns, I start reading his or her palms, using the person's hands as well as the palm print. I always read the hands in a set order. I start by looking at the four major lines in the order of heart, head, life, then destiny. I then examine the thumb and fingers, followed by the mounts. After this, I look at the minor lines and markings. I use the information I've gained from the initial examination of the hands and the dermatoglyphics to help me decide what to say while doing this examination.

Usually, the client will start asking questions or make other comments while I'm doing this. If they're reticent, I encourage them by saying something along the lines of "Does that sound right?" or "Would you agree with that?"

By this time, it's usually obvious why they've come for a reading. Often, they can't wait to tell me what their problem is. Only occasionally do I need to ask them if they have any specific questions.

If the person is seeking help or advice, I then start focusing on whatever their major area of concern is. At this stage, even if the client has been quiet until now, the reading will turn into a conversation, and I can concentrate on examining the palms and answering his or her questions to the best of my ability.

If the person has come for help in choosing a suitable career or wants to know if he or she should pursue a particular skill or talent, I'll focus on that.

Your goal should be to help your clients as much as you can and to have them leave feeling empowered and more positive about the future than they were when they came in.

A Sample Reading

Here is an example of a brief reading for a woman in her early forties. The palmistry indications for what I told her are in parentheses. The first thing I noticed is the shape and feel of her hands. Her hand is fire-shaped, fleshy, but firm, with strong mounts of Venus and Luna.

"You're enthusiastic, creative, and versatile. You get excited about things that interest you, and that sometimes seems to be almost everything! Details are not your strong point. You seem to prefer the overall view and get bogged down if there are too many details. You need plenty of variety in your life and sometimes lose interest before you've completed some of the things you start (this is all from her fire hand). You're a born leader and enjoy being in charge (fire hand, plus long Jupiter finger).

Figure 38: Sample Hand

"You have an interesting heart line. There are two basic types of heart lines and you're a mixture of the two. That's indicated by this fork. The main line carries on in a straight line, while the other branch curves and finishes in the ideal spot between your first and second fingers. This gives you the ability to see both sides of a situation. The emotional side of your life hasn't always been easy (chains and islands on the line), but it looks as if you're not quite the same person you used to be, and that area of your life will be much easier in the future than it has been in the past. You've learned from experience and aren't as romantic as you used to be. You can fall in love easily, but your head will always have something to say (fork on the heart line).

"You have a strong and long head line. This shows that you're a good thinker, and if something really interests you, you want to know as much about it as you can. It curves slightly and heads toward this area known as the mount of Luna. This gives you a good imagination. There's a pronounced gap between your head line and your life line where they start. This shows that you've always been very independent. You can be impulsive at times, too, and—I don't know if you realize it yet—you're becoming more outspoken the older you get (gap between head and life lines).

"Your life line is clear and well-marked. As you can see it comes halfway across your palm, so you've plenty of energy and stamina at your disposal. You worry a bit at times, but it looks as if your more serious worries are in the past (worry lines inside life line).

"Your destiny line is strong, clear, and well-marked. It starts away from your life line, which is another sign of your independent spirit. People with a destiny line like yours usually follow a specific career. However, at the moment you're in this area here (the quadrangle). As you can see, your destiny line is shadowed by another line. They are covering, or protecting, each other, and this shows you're doing some important thinking about where you want to go from here. It looks as if you'll be changing direction slightly. I'll go into that a bit more later.

"You have a long, strong thumb. You're easy to get along with but can be stubborn at times. Once your mind's been made up, it would be hard for anyone to try to change it. You certainly know how to stand up for yourself (stiff thumb and firm mounts of Mars).

"The second section of your thumb is quite a bit longer than the tip section. This means that you get great ideas but don't always feel the need to do them all. This doesn't matter too much, though, as you seem to always be full of ideas, and you have enough energy and ambition to take advantage of the best ones (broad hand, strong destiny and head lines, long index finger, and fire hand).

"You have a passionate nature (large, firm mount of Venus). Obviously, this relates partly to your love life, but it also means you put a great deal of passion and enthusiasm into everything you do.

"You have strong leadership potential and invariably get your own way in the end (long index finger). You should always aim high. I think people have always looked to you to take charge and be the leader.

"You have a strong, straight little finger. Can you see that it's set low compared to the other fingers? This means that everything in your life will go well for a while, and then you'll get dumped into something and need to climb out again. It's learning the hard way, learning from experience. It also means everything takes longer than you would like (the space between her head and life lines means she always wants quick results).

"Can you see how your little finger is held apart from the other fingers? This is another sign that you're an independent thinker. You like to make up your own mind and take little on trust. You have a good tip section on your little finger. This means you communicate well with others using your voice.

"Your ring finger is the finger of creativity and beautiful things. You have a good middle section on this finger, which shows you have natural good taste. You'd do well in a career that involves dealing with anything you find attractive (middle phalange of ring finger and tip phalange of the little finger). You're basically honest (straight little finger) and would find it hard to sell anything you didn't personally like.

"The next finger (middle finger) relates to limitations and balance. It should be the longest finger on your hand and it should be as straight as possible. Yours curves very slightly toward your third finger. This means you may have underrated yourself creatively when you were young.

"Your index (Jupiter) finger is longer than your ring (Apollo) finger. This gives you plenty of drive and ambition. It could even mean that you sometimes feel there's something inside you forcing you on to greater and greater achievement. This is good, but you need to make sure you allow enough time to relax and unwind. I think you've learned how to do this (lack of stress lines and few strain lines).

"The bottom section of all your fingers is padded (I actually mean slightly soft and spongy to the touch, but padded sounds better). This shows that you enjoy food and may well be a good cook.

"You have a good money sign (triangle created by the destiny line, head line, and a minor line). This shows you have the potential to do well financially. However, as I'm sure you've discovered, it comes with a great deal of hard work and effort (line bisecting the triangle and the dropped little finger). You'll also inherit some money during your life (curving line under Apollo finger), but most of your money will be earned. Fortunately, people with fire hands are usually pretty shrewd when it comes to money, so I'm sure you'll be able to hang on to some of the money that comes in (long little finger and closed money triangle).

"You have a good line of intuition, and it looks as if you act on your feelings, at least some of the time (well-marked line of intuition). This can't always be easy, as most of the time you're in such a hurry that you may not stop long enough to listen. It's good that you do pause every now and again because your intuition will keep you on track.

"You're loyal to family and friends. You're also kind and generous (heart line well away from the base of the fingers and wide quadrangle on percussion side of the palm). Fortunately, you're also strong and able to stand up for yourself. You won't let anyone take advantage of your good nature.

"All of those things are useful in your career as well as in your personal life. Speaking of career, you need to be in charge. With your strong index finger, long thumb, and powerful destiny line, you would ideally be self-employed. This is aided by your straight little finger and this line here (hepatica) that heads toward it. If you're not, you should be in a senior role in someone else's business, but in that situation, you'd need a great deal of autonomy.

"You should also be working in a field that deals with something you really like (second phalange of Apollo and good mount of Luna). It also should be dealing directly with the public as this is something you're very good at (tip section of little finger, loops on fingerprints, and loop of humor).

"Looking at your destiny line, I'd say you're contemplating a slight change in the nature of your work. You probably haven't made that change yet (because she's come for a reading), but it's not far away. It looks as if your destiny line is changing. In the future it looks as if it will be heading toward your ring finger (the new branch of her destiny line). This is the creative finger, so potentially you'll be in a creative field. You have a good creative curve which helps that, too (as does the mount of Luna).

"Your strong mount of Venus could have you doing some form of decorating—interior design, perhaps. However, your padded fingers show you may well be working with food. If it's not your career, it's certainly an important interest."

While reading this lady's palm, I thought she was probably running a restaurant. This was from her broad hand, strong destiny line, long index finger, padded third phalanges, and creative curve. Her hands were smooth and showed no calluses or other signs of manual work. It occurred to me that she might have been a chef who'd moved into management or maybe owned her own restaurant or catering business.

It turned out that she had always loved baking. She started her career after gaining certification in baking and pastry arts. Her first job was working for a large hotel who paid for her to learn cake decorating. Unfortunately, they gave her no opportunities to practice and develop this new skill and she became frustrated. After a couple of years, she left the hotel to work for a wholesale cake company. Her leadership skills were quickly recognized and within a year she was in charge of the factory. She was happy as it gave her a chance to use her leadership skills, but she spent most of her days in an office rather than doing what she loved: the baking and decorating. However, the money was good and the corporation treated her well, so she stayed there for many years.

Her marriage had broken up about a year before she came to see me, and as a result of that, she had a small sum of money that she planned to use to start her own cake decorating company. She'd already decided to do this and came to see me looking for confirmation that it was a good idea.

As you can see, a great deal of information can be provided in a quick reading using just the person's major hand. Obviously, in a full-length reading, I'd examine both hands in much more detail. I'd also be able to time events more accurately using dividers on the palm print, and I'd use a magnifying glass to examine the dermatoglyphics.

Also, of course, almost all readings are conversations rather than monologues. I did this reading some years ago and can't remember exactly what she or I said at the time. The one thing I vividly remember is her eyes widening when I said that her strong mount of Venus indicates she'd be good at decorating.

This lady started her new business only weeks after her reading. I wasn't surprised that it was a success from the very start. She managed to get publicity on local television when her store opened by presenting the news team with a cake to congratulate them on a good piece of reporting. She continues to get publicity every now and again when she produces seasonal cakes. She's extremely busy, with no time to even think about a new life partner, but she's happy, fulfilled, and doing exactly what she was born to do.

Ethics

All of your readings should be caring, helpful, and empathetic. Your goal should be to give palm readings that will improve the quality of your clients' lives. Consequently, you need to treat your clients with respect. You must be tactful and choose your words with care. If you're a compassionate person, you won't need to concern yourself too much about this as you'll do the right thing automatically. However, everyone makes mistakes at times, and you should think about what you are prepared to say and do during the course of a reading.

Doctors, attorneys, psychologists, and social workers are all bound by a strict code of ethics. There is no governing board that regulates palmists or other types of readers. Consequently, you need to make up your own mind on what standards you'll follow.

Confidentiality is essential. If your client feels comfortable and safe discussing anything at all with you, he or she is more likely to be honest and tell you everything that's relevant to his or her concern. This means you can help your client much more than you can if he or she doesn't feel comfortable enough to tell you the whole story. In certain situations, you might be the only person in the whole world that your client can talk to about his or her concern. Can you imagine how devastated your client would be if you told other people about the client's concerns and he or she found out about it?

Clients come to you for help. Sometimes their problems are horrendous. I've read for people who've made bad mistakes or have been emotionally hurt. I've read for people who've done horrible things to others. I've read the hands of many victims and heard some unbelievably distressing stories. No matter what you hear, you're not there to judge your clients. Your task is to listen to them, help them, and encourage them as much as you can. You need to remain open-minded, non-judgmental, and impartial no matter what your clients tell you. If appropriate, you should refer clients to a qualified professional or agency for further help. You should always do this if your clients ask you for medical, legal, psychological, or financial advice.

Don't predict deaths or accidents. Even if you're convinced that you can see something on the client's hands that indicates this, you may be wrong. For instance, I've seen many elderly people with short life lines. I've even read the palms of a fifty-year-old man who had no visible life lines. Some people would consider a short life line or the lack of a life line to indicate an early death, which obviously didn't occur in these cases. Also, as people's hands change over the course of their lives, what may look worrying now, may look completely different a few months or years later. It's irresponsible to predict death and accidents, and it causes your clients unnecessary stress and worry. Your focus should be on providing positive information rather than negative.

Don't tell your clients what to do. Discuss with them what you read in their palms and offer advice and help. Ultimately, though, they have to take responsibility for their own lives and this includes making their own decisions.

Help your clients to be independent and stand on their own two feet. Every reader gets clients who want to consult with them every time they have to make a decision of any sort. This isn't good for you or the client.

It's not appropriate to become romantically or sexually involved with any of your clients. You need to make sure that your feelings and desires play no part in your readings. If you feel attracted to a client, or a client expresses feelings for you, you must handle the situation professionally. If necessary, stop the reading, refund their money if they've paid in advance, and refer them to another reader.

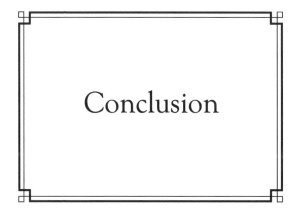

Conclusion

It's amazing how many people aren't aware of or using the talents or potential they were born with. Helping people discover these is one of the most valuable things you could possibly do for them. It's also incredibly satisfying.

While reading this book you might have discovered talents you possess but haven't developed yet. Once you start using these natural talents, every aspect of your life will improve. Your enthusiasm and creativity will increase, as you'll discover you're naturally good at whatever it happens to be. You'll feel happy, fulfilled, and "in the flow."

Obviously, simply knowing you have a talent isn't enough. You need to be motivated and willing to put in the necessary time and effort to develop it. If you're prepared to pay the price, the rewards can be immeasurable.

If circumstances didn't allow you to develop a particular talent when you were young, the chances are that it's not too late. There are many examples of people taking up new challenges, such as long-distance running, in their fifties or later. Age is not a factor for many talents. You can learn to play the piano at any age. You probably won't get to Carnegie Hall if you start learning at the age of seventy, but you'll still receive a great deal of pleasure and satisfaction every time you sit down to play.

The classic example of someone who started using her talent late in life is Grandma Moses (1860–1961), the famous American folk artist. She discovered her talent for painting early when she was a teenager but certain circumstances meant she wasn't able to take it up seriously until she was seventy-eight. She was a prolific artist who produced more than 1,500 paintings. In 2006, one of her paintings sold for $1,200,000.00.

An old saying that has been attributed to many people goes like this: "Do what you love and you'll never have to work a day in your life." With your palmistry skills, you can help people to feel good about themselves and to do what they love. I hope you'll also do this for yourself.

Study everything you can find on palmistry and read as many palms as you can. It's the best way to improve your palmistry skills, and you'll learn something from every palm you read.

I wish you great success with your palm reading skills.

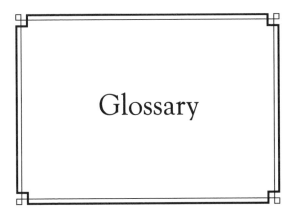

Glossary

Air hand: The palm of the air hand is square or slightly oblong, and the fingers are long. People with air hands are imaginative, conscientious, thoughtful, and mentally alert.

Angle of generosity: The angle of generosity is the angle created between the thumb and the side of the palm and index finger when the thumb is extended. The wider this angle is, the more generous and open-minded the person will be.

Apollo finger: The Apollo finger is the ring finger. It's named after Apollo, the Greek god of the sun. It's sometimes called the Uranus finger. Apollo was a complex god who looked after many things, including music, art, and knowledge. Consequently, the Apollo finger relates to the aesthetic side of life.

Arch: The arch is one of the three main types of fingerprint patterns. People with arches in their fingerprints are conscientious, practical, and loyal.

Break: A break in a line indicates a time when the person's life was disturbed or interrupted. The problem is resolved quickly if the two lines overlap. However, if there is a pronounced gap with no overlap, the problem can affect the person's health as well as the qualities of the line until the line starts again.

Chain: Chains are made up of a series of islands or ovals on a line. They indicate anxiety, stress, and strain in the area of life indicated by the line they appear on.

Conic hand: A conic shaped hand is graceful and has a curved appearance. The palm is oblong and fleshy, and the fingers are long with rounded tips.

Consistency: Some hands are hard and resistant to pressure, while others appear soft and spongy. This is called hand consistency. People with firm hands are energetic and enjoy keeping busy. People with soft hands lack energy and motivation.

Dermatoglyphics: Dermatoglyphics is the study of the fine skin ridge patterns on the surface of the palm and fingers. The best-known examples of these are fingerprints.

Destiny line: The destiny line is a major line that runs from the base of the palm toward the fingers. It provides a sense of direction to the person's life.

Earth hand: The earth hand has a square palm and short fingers. The lines on the palm are few, but they're deep and well-marked. People with earth hands are practical, reliable, responsible, and cautious.

Elementary hand: The elementary hand has a square palm and short, stubby fingers. The skin is coarse, and the palm has few lines on it.

Fire hand: The fire hand consists of an oblong palm and short fingers. People with fire hands are enthusiastic, versatile, impatient, and excitable.

Flexibility: The flexibility of the hand can be determined by resting the back of the person's palm on your fingertips and pressing against his or her fingertips with your thumb. The fingers may bend down slightly, easily, or be totally resistant to pressure. The flexibility of the hand relates to the flexibility of the person's mind.

Girdle of Venus: The girdle of Venus is a line or series of lines that runs parallel to the heart line for part of its length, between the heart line and the fingers. People who have this line are extremely sensitive.

Head line: The head line is a major line that runs across the palm, starting attached to or close to the life line. This line reveals the quality of the person's intellect and way of thinking.

Heart line: The heart line is a major line that runs across the palm near the base of the fingers. It starts at the side of the palm beneath the little finger and ends under the index or middle fingers or, more usually, between them. It reveals the person's emotional life.

Hepatica: The hepatica runs diagonally across the palm from inside the life line close to the wrist and finishes near the start of the heart line. It is not as clearly marked as the four main lines. It reveals the person's health. Many people don't have a hepatica, and this is a sign of extremely good health.

Intuition line: The line of intuition is a short line about one inch long that starts on the fleshy mound at the base of the percussion side of the hand and heads in an arc toward the center of the palm. It shows that the person is intuitive and acts on his or her hunches and feelings.

Island: An island in a line indicates stress, strain, and tension. A number of islands form a chain, which indicates the problems continue for the length of time indicated by the chain.

Jupiter finger: The index finger is known as the Jupiter finger. It is named after the Roman god Jupiter and relates to confidence, assertiveness, leadership, and self-esteem.

Knotty fingers: "Knotty fingers" is the term used to describe fingers with prominent knuckles.

Life line: The life line is the major line that encircles the thumb and reveals how much energy and vitality the person has at his or her disposal.

Loop: The loop is a skin ridge pattern, oval or round in shape, that is found on the fingerprints or the palm of the hand. People with loops in their fingerprints are versatile, adaptable, and work well with others.

Medical stigmata: The medical stigmata is a group of three or four fine vertical lines immediately below the little finger. People with these lines often choose careers that involve helping others.

Mercury finger: The little, or pinky, finger is named after Mercury, the Roman messenger of the gods. This finger relates to communication, finance, and commerce.

Mounts: There are nine mounts on the hand, all named after planets. They are usually raised areas on the surface of the palm. The quality and quantity of these reveal what the person is interested in.

Percussion: The percussion is the outer edge of the palm between the wrist and little finger. It gained this name as many percussion instruments are played by striking them with this side of the palm.

Phalange: A phalange is one section of a finger or thumb. The fingernail phalange relates to the spiritual aspects of life. The middle phalange relates to the person's intellect, and the base phalange, closest to the palm, relates to the material aspects of life.

Philosophical hand: The philosophical hand has a square palm and long fingers with pronounced knuckles on the joints. Because of this, the philosophical hand is often called a knotty hand. People with knotty hands are deep thinkers who enjoy analyzing everything. They're cultured, knowledgeable, and easy to get along with.

Psychic hand: The psychic hand and fingers are long, slender, and graceful. People with psychic hands are idealistic, intuitive, and are usually impractical.

Quadrangle: The quadrangle is the area of the palm between the head and heart lines.

Rascettes: Rascettes are sometimes known as bracelets. They are the lines that cross the wrist at the base of the palm. Most people have three of them. In the past, many people believed that each rascette represented twenty-five years of life.

Relationship lines: The relationship lines, sometimes known as marriage or affection lines, are fine horizontal lines on the side of the palm immediately below the little finger. Well-marked lines indicate a permanent, or at least a long-term, relationship.

Ring of Solomon: The ring of Solomon is a fine semi-circular line that partially or wholly surrounds the base of the index finger. People with this ring have a desire to serve humanity as well as a strong interest in psychic matters.

Saturn finger: The middle finger is usually the longest finger on the hand. It's called the Saturn finger after the Roman god of agriculture. It relates to responsibility, duty, caution, and common-sense.

Simian crease: The simian crease occurs when the heart and head lines appear as a single line that runs across the palm.

Sister line: The sister line is a line that doubles another line on the palm. This second line adds strength and protection to the first line. The most common example of this is a sister line to the life line, which even has its own name—the line of Mars.

Smooth fingers: Smooth fingers do not have prominent joints, and appear smooth throughout their length.

Spatulate hand: In a spatulate hand the palm and some of the fingertips are shaped like a spatula. The palm is almost rectangular-shaped but is broader, either at the wrist or immediately below the fingers. Spatulate fingers flare slightly at the tips. People with spatulate hands are enthusiastic, energetic, and have a need to be busy and active.

Square hand: The square or practical hand has a square palm and medium-length fingers. It contains an angle of practicality. People with square hands are patient, conscientious, determined, and honest. They lack diplomatic skills and sometimes find themselves in hot water by saying what's on their minds.

Sun line: The Sun line is a fine line that parallels the destiny line for part of its length and ends close to the mount of Apollo, the raised mount, below the ring finger. Because of this, it's sometimes called the line of Apollo. It's a fortunate line to have as it's a sign of ultimate success.

Travel lines: Travel lines are fine lines between the heart line and the wrist on the percussion side of the palm. They are sometimes called restlessness lines as people with them have restless natures that can be satisfied with travel.

Tri-radii: Tri-radii are sometimes called apexes. They are small triangles created by the skin ridge patterns and usually look like a three-pointed star. Most people have four to six tri-radii on their palms and fingers.

Via lasciva: The via lasciva is a straight horizontal line that starts on the percussion side of the palm about three quarters of the way down the palm from the base of the little finger. People with this line have a constant need for something exciting to look forward to.

Water hand: The water hand consists of an oblong palm and long fingers. People with water hands are sensitive, sympathetic, idealistic, and impressionable.

Whorls: Whorls are concentric circles inside the fingerprints. People with these are independent, original, and individualistic.

Worry lines: Worry lines are fine lines that radiate outward across the mount of Venus (the mound at the base of the thumb) toward the life line. Most are unimportant, but they can affect the person's health if they cross the life line.

Suggested Reading

Altman, Nathaniel and Andrew Fitzherbert. *Career, Success and Self-Fulfilment*. Wellingborough, UK: The Aquarian Press, 1988.

Altman, Nathaniel. *Palmistry: The Universal Guide*. New York: Sterling Publishing Company, Inc., 2009.

d'Arpentigny, Stanislaus. *La chirognamie, ou l'art de reconnaître les tendances d'intelligence d'après les forms de la main*. Paris: Charles Le Clere, 1843. Published in English as *The Science of the Hand*, translated by Ed Heron-Allen. London and New York: Ward, Lock & Bowden, 1865.

Asano, Hachiro. *Hands: The Complete Book of Palmistry*. Tokyo: Japan Publications, Inc., 1985.

Bashir, Mir. *The Art of Hand Analysis*. London: Frederick Muller Limited, 1973.

Benham, William G. *The Laws of Scientific Hand Reading*. New York: Duell, Sloan and Pearce, 1900. Revised edition 1946.

Benham, William G. *How to Choose Vocations from the Hand*. New York: G. P. Putnam's Sons, 1932.

Brandon-Jones, David. *Practical Palmistry*. London: Rider and Company, 1981.

Brandon-Jones, David and Veronica Bennett. *Your Hand and Your Career*. London: Arrow Books, 1980.

Campbell, Edward D. *The Encyclopedia of Palmistry*. New York: Perigee Books, 1996.

Coburn, Ronelle. *Destiny at Your Fingertips: Discover the Inner Purpose of Your Life and What It Takes to Live It*. Woodbury, MN: Llewellyn Publications, 2008.

Coyle, Daniel. *The Talent Code: Unlocking the Secret of Skill in Math, Art, Music, Sport, and Just about Everything Else*. New York: Random House, Inc., 2009.

Cummins, Harold, and Charles Midlo. *Fingerprints, Palms and Soles*. New York: Dover Publications, 1943.

Fincham, Jonny. *The Spellbinding Power of Palmistry: New Insights into an Ancient Art*. Sutton Mallet, UK: Green Magic, 2005.

Fitzherbert, Andrew. *Hand Psychology*. North Ryde, AU: Angus & Robertson Publishers, 1986.

Fuda, Peter. *Leadership Transformed: How Ordinary Managers Become Extraordinary Leaders*. Boston, MA: Houghton Mifflin Harcourt Publishing Company, 2013.

Galton, Francis. *Fingerprints*. New York: Da Capo Press, 1965.

Gettings, Fred. *The Book of the Hand*. London: Hamlyn Books, 1965.

Harwig, Kathryn. *The Millenium Effect*. St. Paul, MN: Spring Press, 1996.

Hipskind, Judith. *Palmistry: The Whole View*. St. Paul, MN: Llewellyn Publications, 1977.

Holtzman, Arnold. *The Illustrated Textbook of Psychodiagnostic Chirology in Analysis and Therapy*. Toronto, ON: Greenwood-Chase Press, 2004.

Hutchinson, Beryl. *Your Life in Your Hands*. London: Neville Spearman, 1967.

Jaquin, Noel. *The Hand of Man*. London: Faber & Faber Limited, 1933.

——— *The Human Hand: The Living Symbol*. London: Rockliff Publishing, 1956.

Lutz, Bob. *Icons and Idiots: Straight Talk on Leadership*. New York: Penguin Group (USA) Inc., 2013.

Lyon, Sheila and Mark Sherman. *Palms Up! A Handy Guide to 21st-Century Palmistry*. New York: Berkley Books, 2005.

Manning, John. *The Finger Ratio: Sex, Behaviour and Disease Revealed in the Fingers*. London: Faber & Faber Limited, 2008.

Martin, Ron. *Palm Readers Notebook*. Manassas, VA: Ron Martin, 1993.

Masters, Anthony. *Mind Map*. London: Eyre Methuen Ltd., 1980.

Nakagaichi, Mika. *Palmistry for the Global Village*. Tokyo: Tachibana Shuppan, 1998.

Nishitani, Yasuto. *Palmistry Revolution: Secret Key to Get Along Successfully*. Tokyo: Tachibana Shuppan Inc., 1992.

Ranald, Josef. *How to Know People by Their Hands*. New York: Modern Age Books, Inc., 1938.

Saint-Germain, Jon. *Runic Palmistry*. St. Paul, MN: Llewellyn Publications, 2001.

Schaumann, Blanka and Alter, Milton. *Dermatoglyphics in Medical Disorders*. New York: Springer-Verlag New York Inc., 1976.

Sherson, R. *The Key to Your Hands*. Auckland, NZ: Mystical Books, 1973.

Spier, Julius. *The Hands of Children: An Introduction to Psycho-Chirology*. London: Kegan Paul, Trench, Trubner & Company, 1944.

St. Hill, Katharine. *The Book of the Hand*. London: Rider & Co., 1927.

Unger, Richard. *Lifeprints: Deciphering Your Life Purpose from Your Fingerprints*. Berkeley: Crossing Press, 2007.

Webster, Richard. *Palm Reading for Beginners*. St. Paul, MN: Llewellyn Publications, 2000.

———. *The Complete Book of Palmistry*. St. Paul, MN: Llewellyn Publications, 2001.

———. *You Can Read Palms*. Woodbury, MN: Llewellyn Publications, 2010.

Wolff, Charlotte. *The Hand in Psychological Diagnosis*. London: Methuen and Company, 1951.

To Write to the Author

If you wish to contact the author or would like more information about this book, please write to the author in care of Llewellyn Worldwide Ltd. and we will forward your request. Both the author and publisher appreciate hearing from you and learning of your enjoyment of this book and how it has helped you. Llewellyn Worldwide Ltd. cannot guarantee that every letter written to the author can be answered, but all will be forwarded. Please write to:

Richard Webster
℅ Llewellyn Worldwide
2143 Wooddale Drive
Woodbury, MN 55125-2989

Please enclose a self-addressed stamped envelope for reply,
or $1.00 to cover costs. If outside the U.S.A., enclose
an international postal reply coupon.

Many of Llewellyn's authors have websites with additional information and resources. For more information, please visit our website at http://www.llewellyn.com.